Label on next page →

D0640715

STAR WARS®

publisher
Mike Richardson

designer
Stephen Reichert

art director
Lia Ribacchi

assisting editor
Dave Marshall

editor
Randy Stradley

The editor gratefully acknowledges the assistance
of Elaine Mederer, Jann Moorhead, David Anderman, Leland Chee,
Sue Rostoni, and Carol Roeder at Lucas Licensing.

Star Wars®: Episode IV — A New Hope
PhotoComic

Published by Dark Horse Books, a division of Dark Horse Comics, Inc.
10956 SE Main Street
Milwaukie, OR 97222

Originally published by TOKYOPOP, Inc.

www.darkhorse.com
www.starwars.com

To find a comics shop in your area,
call the Comic Shop Locator Service toll-free at 1-888-266-4226

First edition: March 2008

ISBN: 978-1-59307-874-4

10 9 8 7 6 5 4 3 2 1

Printed in China

EPISODE IV
A NEW HOPE

STORY AND SCREENPLAY BY
GEORGE LUCAS

DARK HORSE BOOKS®

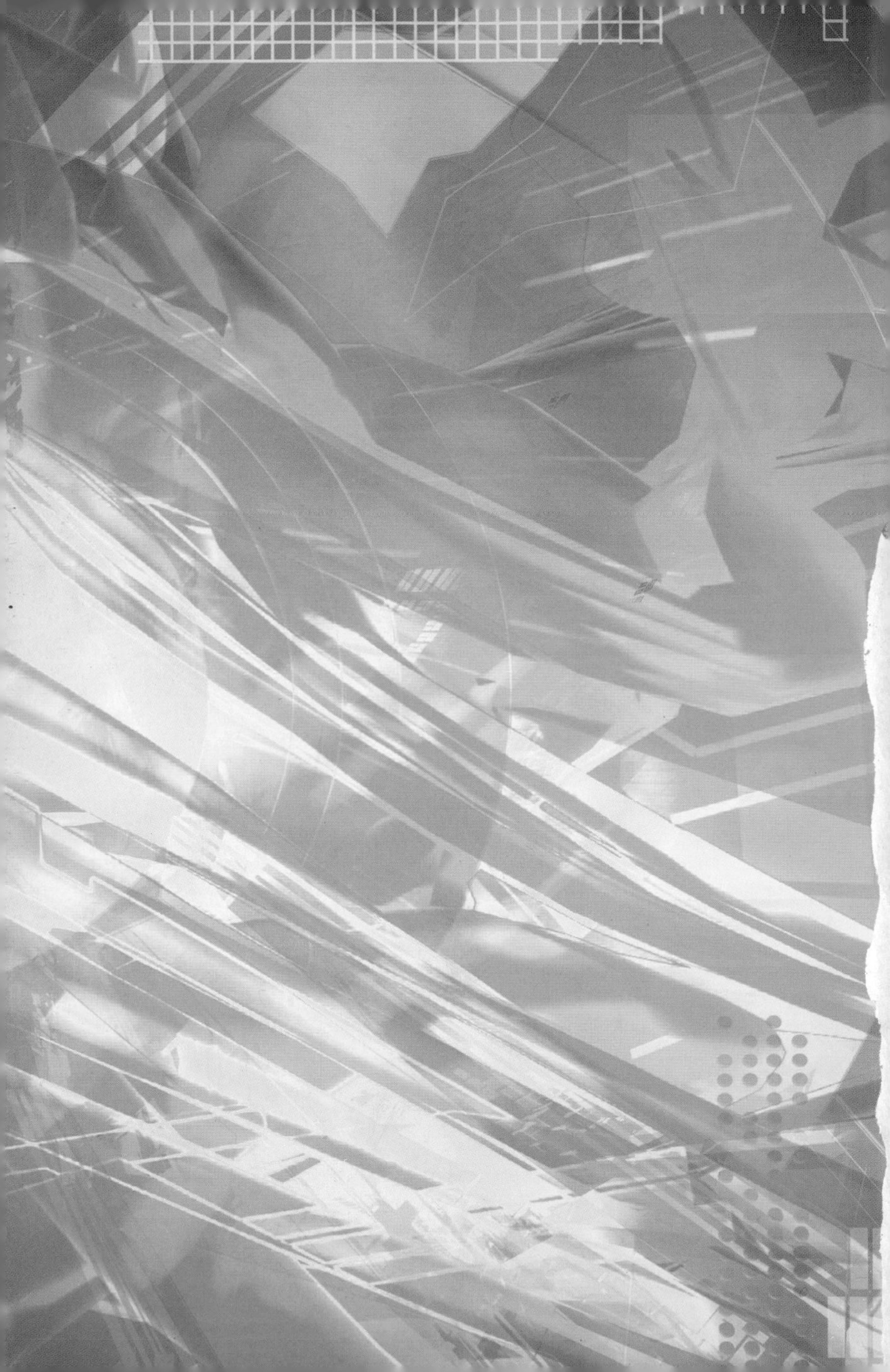

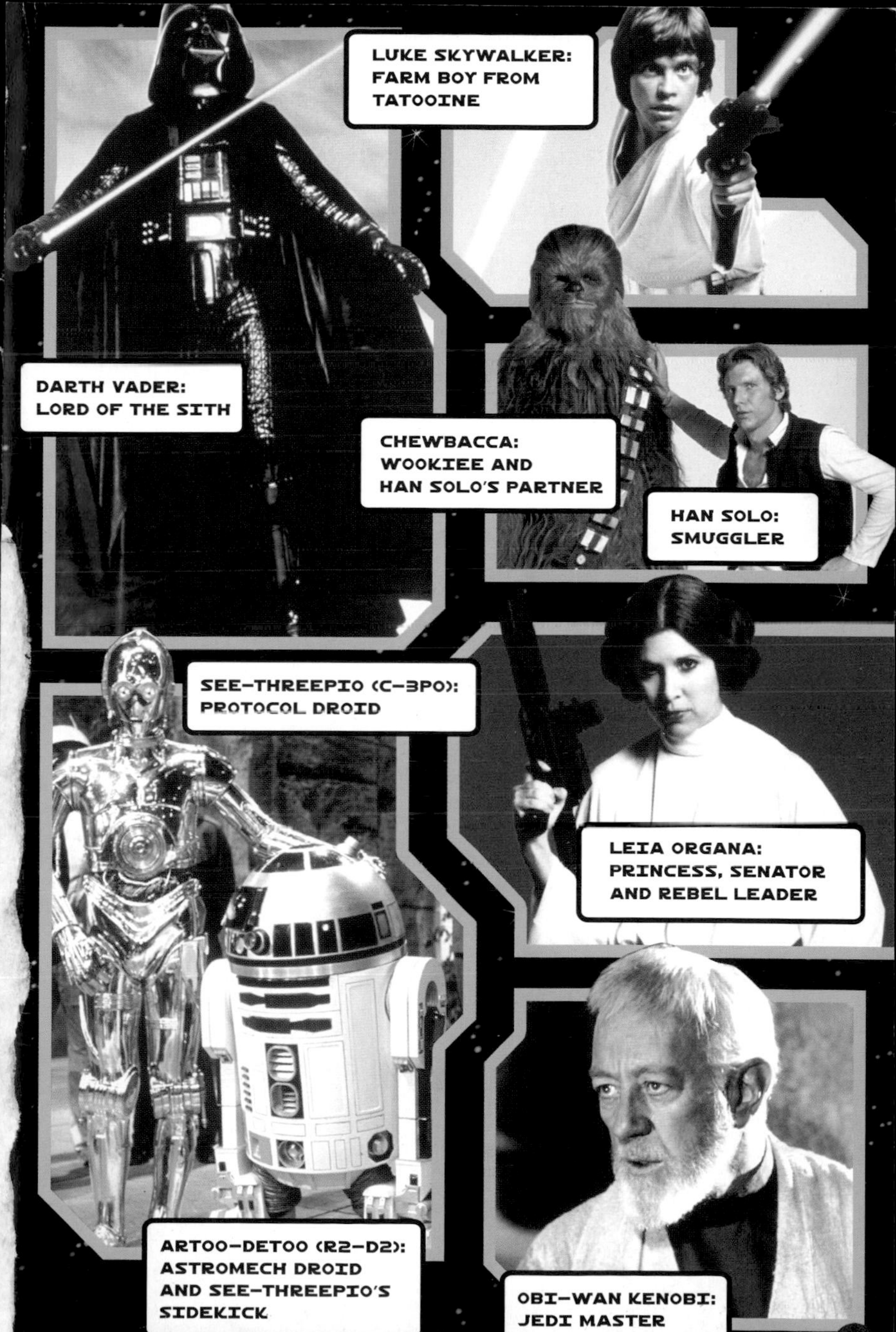
LUKE SKYWALKER: FARM BOY FROM TATOOINE
DARTH VADER: LORD OF THE SITH
CHEWBACCA: WOOKIEE AND HAN SOLO'S PARTNER
HAN SOLO: SMUGGLER
SEE-THREEPIO (C-3PO): PROTOCOL DROID
LEIA ORGANA: PRINCESS, SENATOR AND REBEL LEADER
ARTOO-DETOO (R2-D2): ASTROMECH DROID AND SEE-THREEPIO'S SIDEKICK
OBI-WAN KENOBI: JEDI MASTER

A long time ago in a galaxy far, far away....

It is a period of civil war. Rebel spaceships, striking from a hidden base, have won their first victory against the evil Galactic Empire.

During the battle, Rebel spies managed to steal secret plans to the Empire's ultimate weapon, the Death Star, an armored space station with enough power to destroy an entire planet.

Pursued by the Empire's sinister agents, Princess Leia races home aboard her starship, custodian of the stolen plans that can save her people and restore freedom to the galaxy....

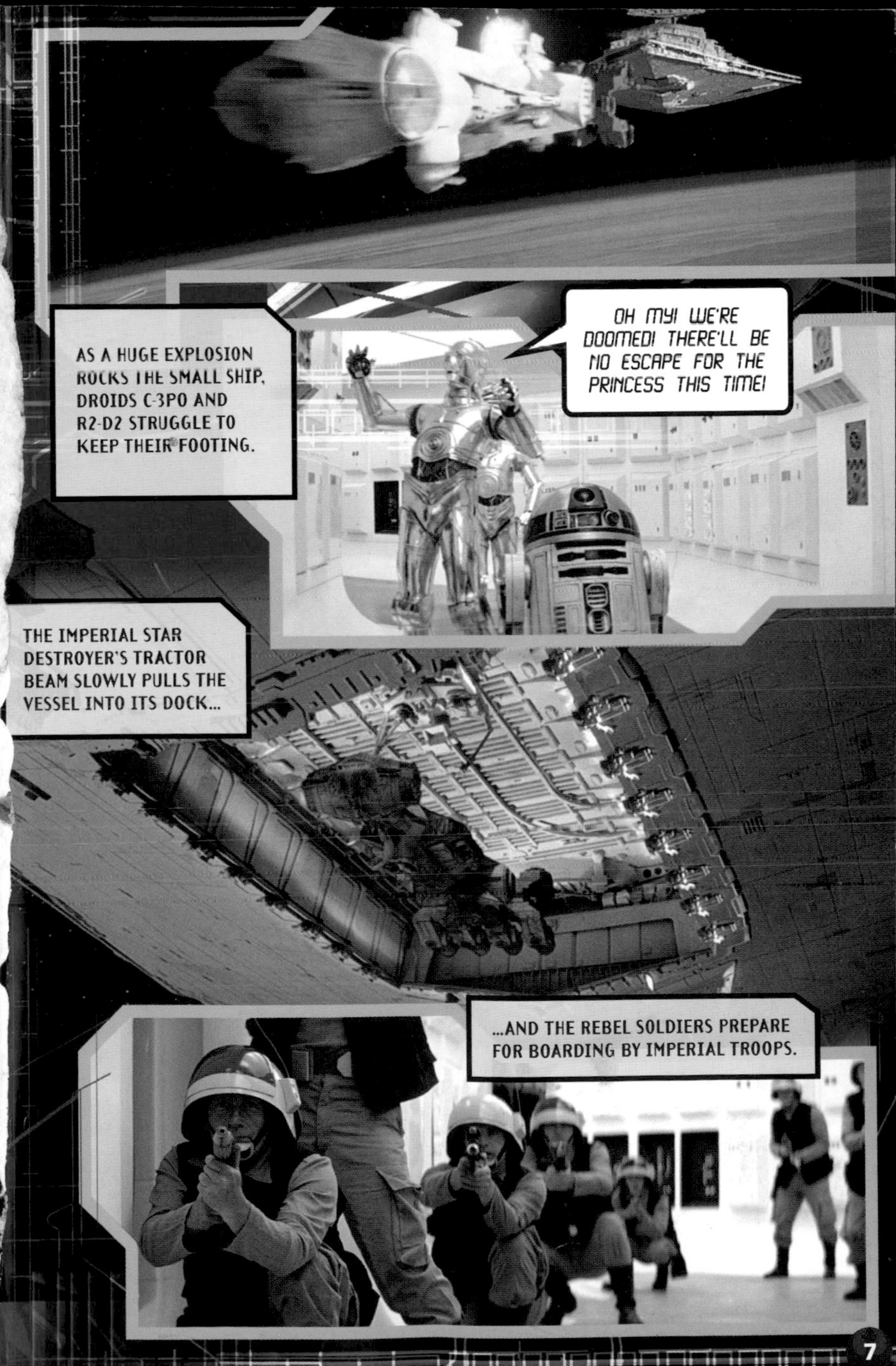
AS A HUGE EXPLOSION ROCKS THE SMALL SHIP, DROIDS C-3PO AND R2-D2 STRUGGLE TO KEEP THEIR FOOTING.
OH MY! WE'RE DOOMED! THERE'LL BE NO ESCAPE FOR THE PRINCESS THIS TIME!
THE IMPERIAL STAR DESTROYER'S TRACTOR BEAM SLOWLY PULLS THE VESSEL INTO ITS DOCK...
...AND THE REBEL SOLDIERS PREPARE FOR BOARDING BY IMPERIAL TROOPS.

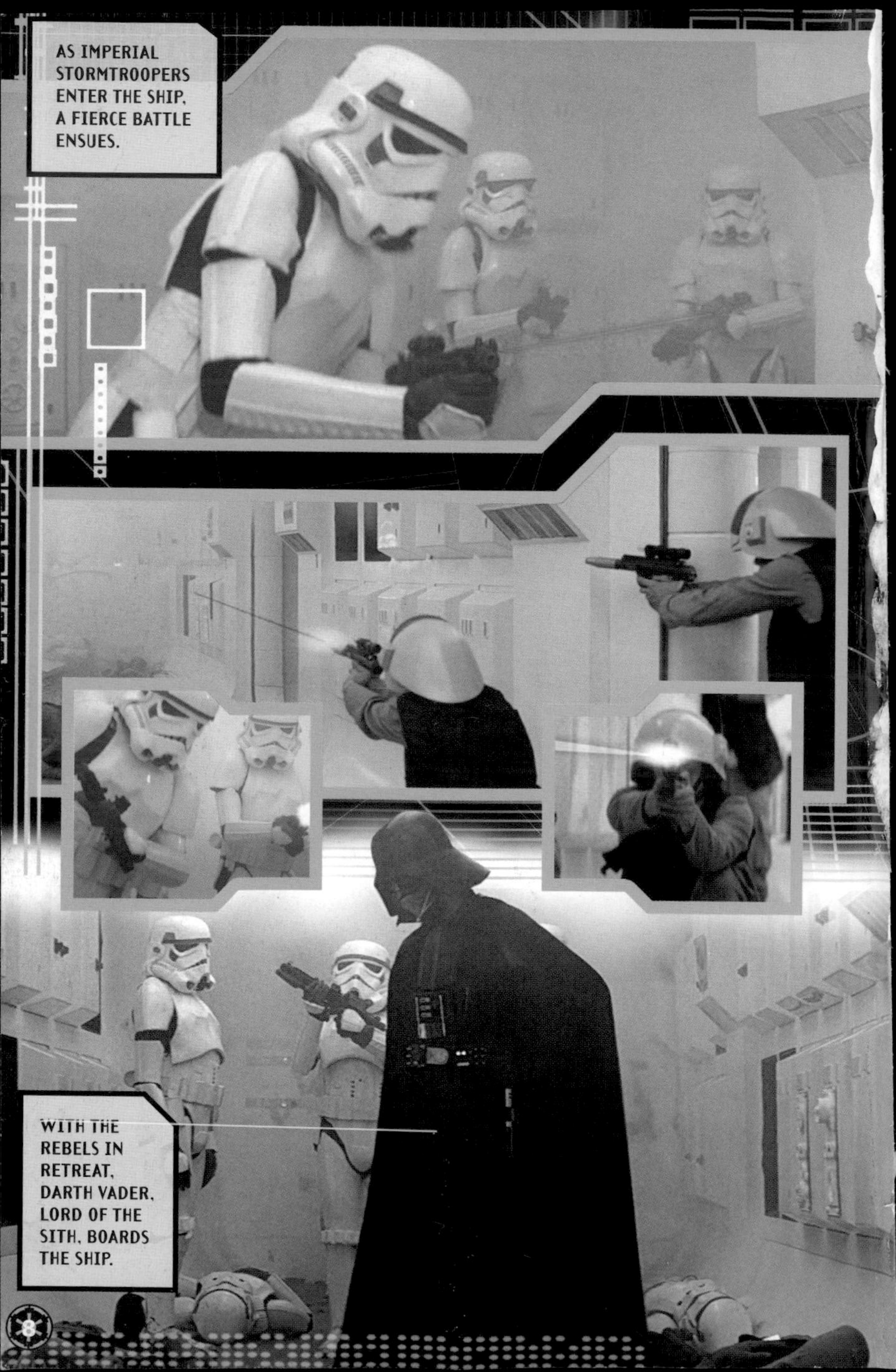

AS IMPERIAL STORMTROOPERS ENTER THE SHIP, A FIERCE BATTLE ENSUES.
WITH THE REBELS IN RETREAT, DARTH VADER, LORD OF THE SITH, BOARDS THE SHIP.

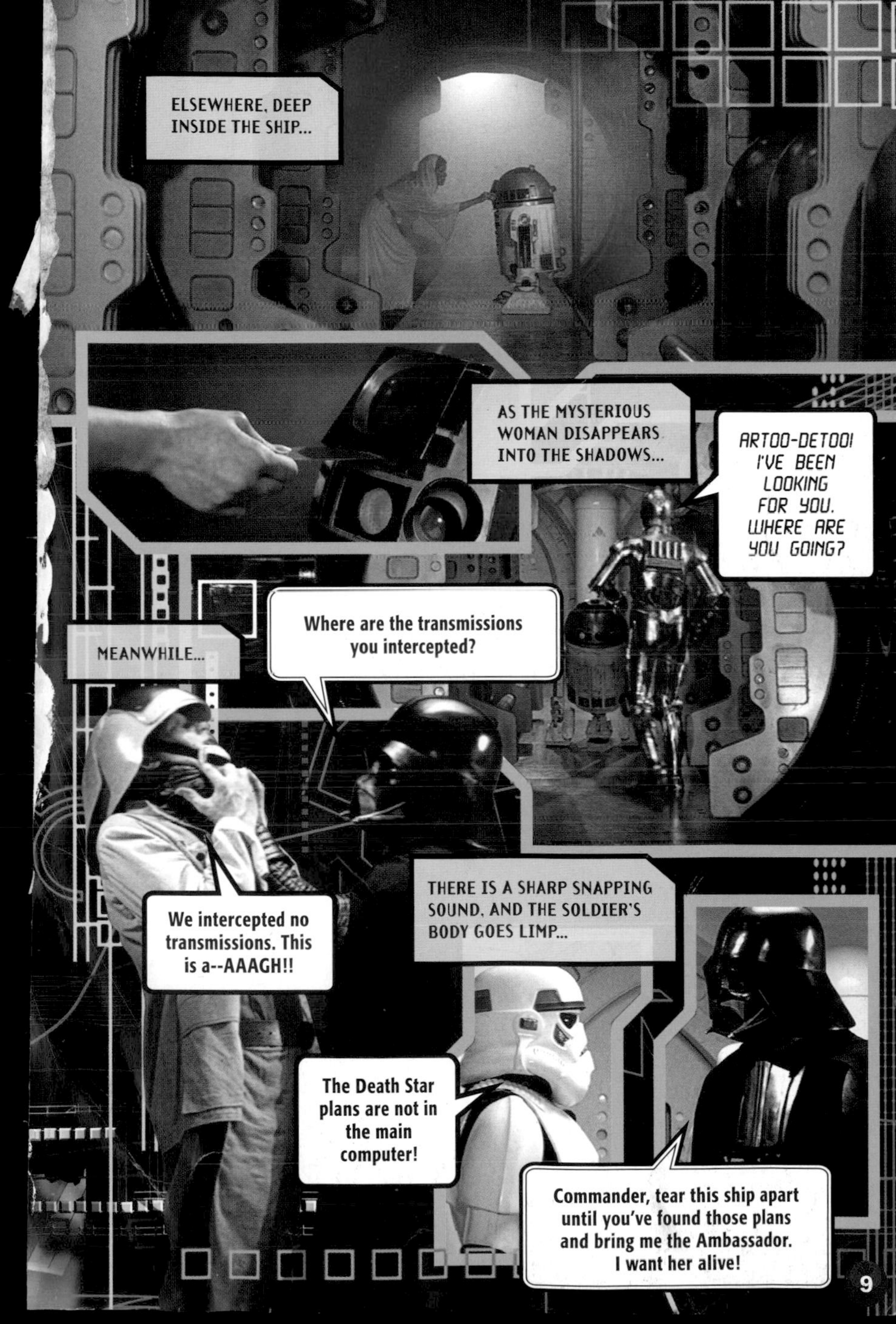

ELSEWHERE, DEEP INSIDE THE SHIP...
AS THE MYSTERIOUS WOMAN DISAPPEARS INTO THE SHADOWS...
ARTOO-DETOO! I'VE BEEN LOOKING FOR YOU. WHERE ARE YOU GOING?
MEANWHILE...
Where are the transmissions you intercepted?
We intercepted no transmissions. This is a--AAAGH!!
THERE IS A SHARP SNAPPING SOUND, AND THE SOLDIER'S BODY GOES LIMP...
The Death Star plans are not in the main computer!
Commander, tear this ship apart until you've found those plans and bring me the Ambassador. I want her alive!

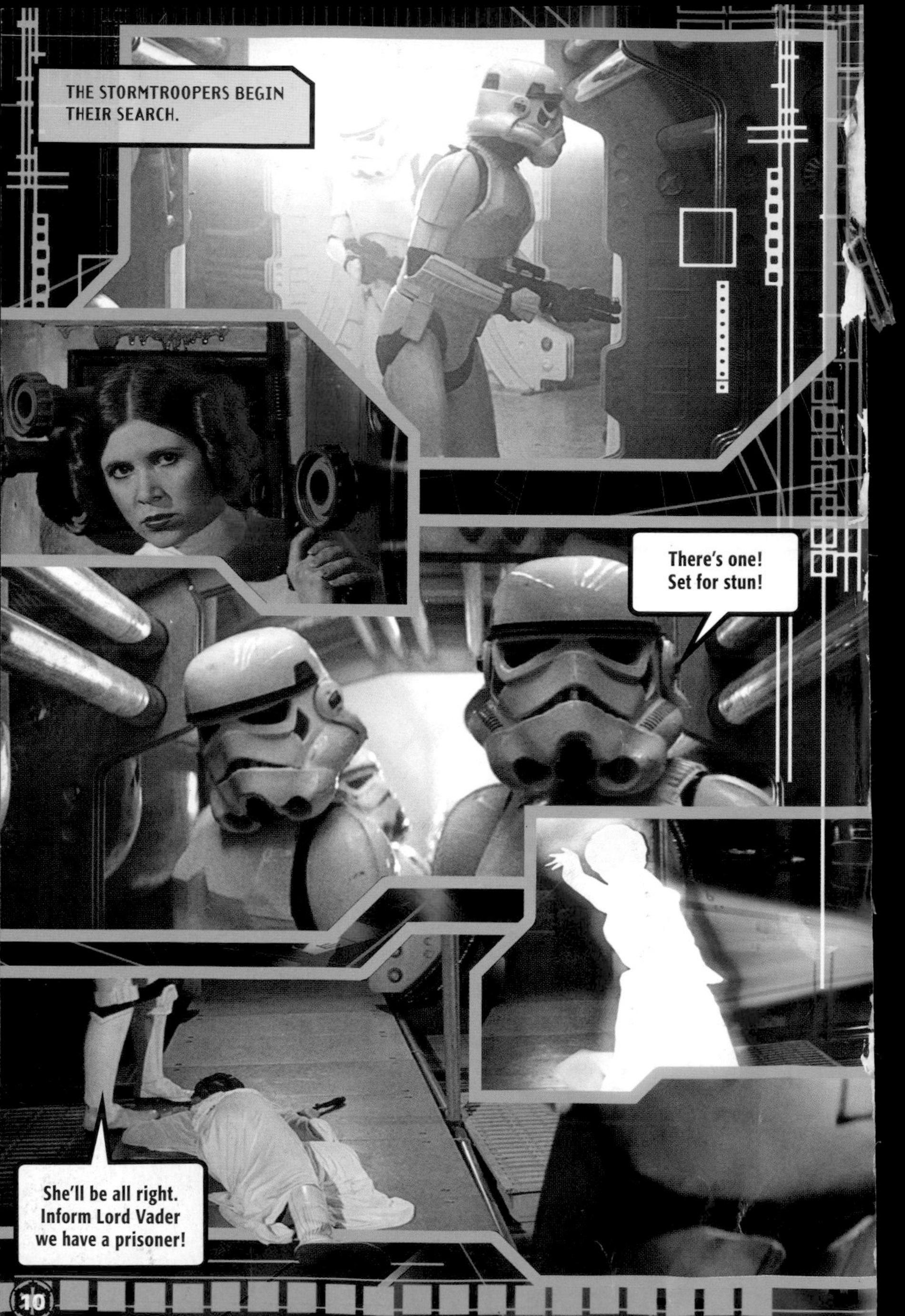
THE STORMTROOPERS BEGIN THEIR SEARCH.
There's one! Set for stun!
She'll be all right. Inform Lord Vader we have a prisoner!

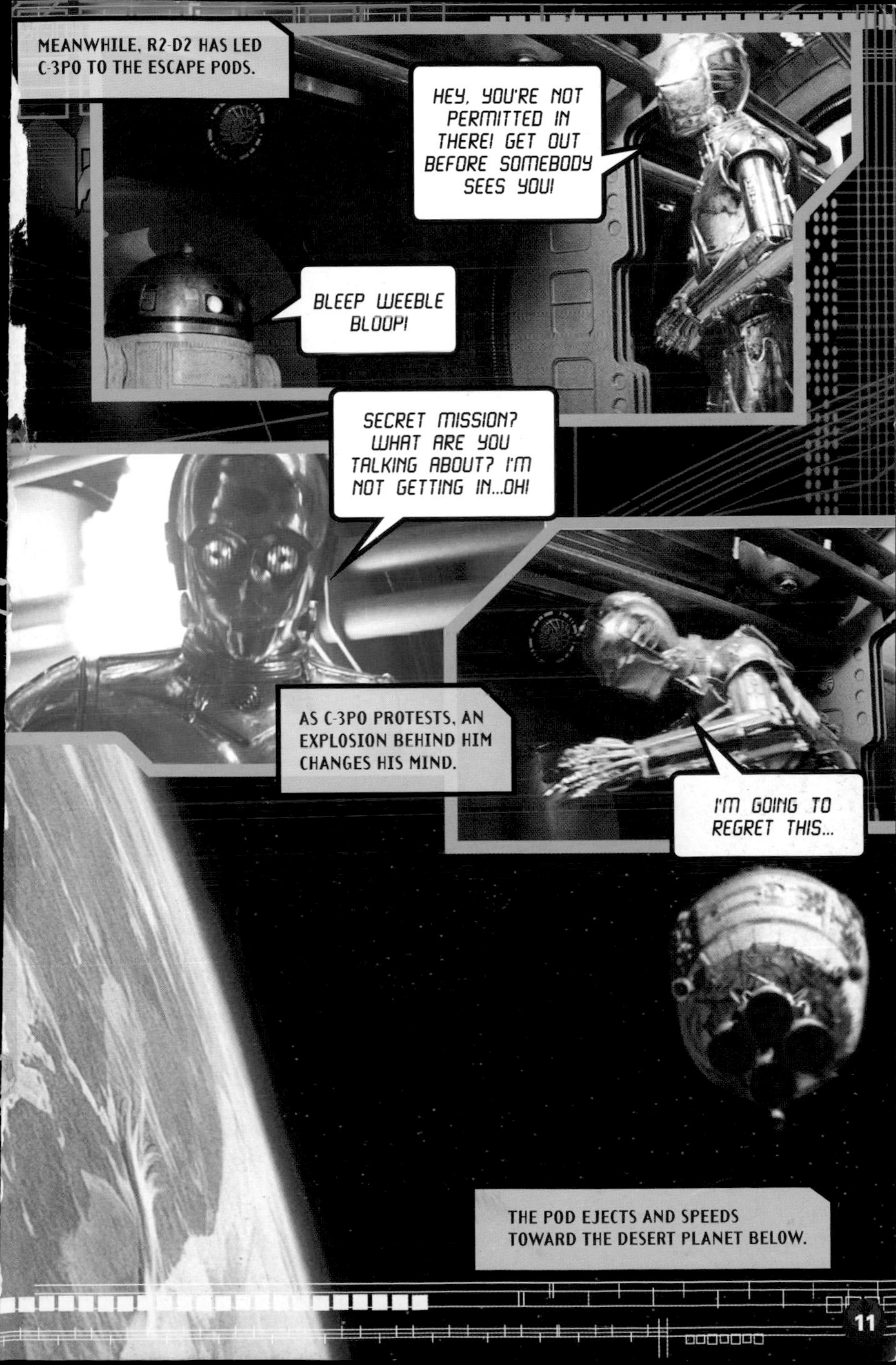
MEANWHILE, R2-D2 HAS LED C-3PO TO THE ESCAPE PODS.
HEY, YOU'RE NOT PERMITTED IN THERE! GET OUT BEFORE SOMEBODY SEES YOU!
BLEEP WEEBLE BLOOP!
SECRET MISSION? WHAT ARE YOU TALKING ABOUT? I'M NOT GETTING IN...OH!
AS C-3PO PROTESTS, AN EXPLOSION BEHIND HIM CHANGES HIS MIND.
I'M GOING TO REGRET THIS...
THE POD EJECTS AND SPEEDS TOWARD THE DESERT PLANET BELOW.

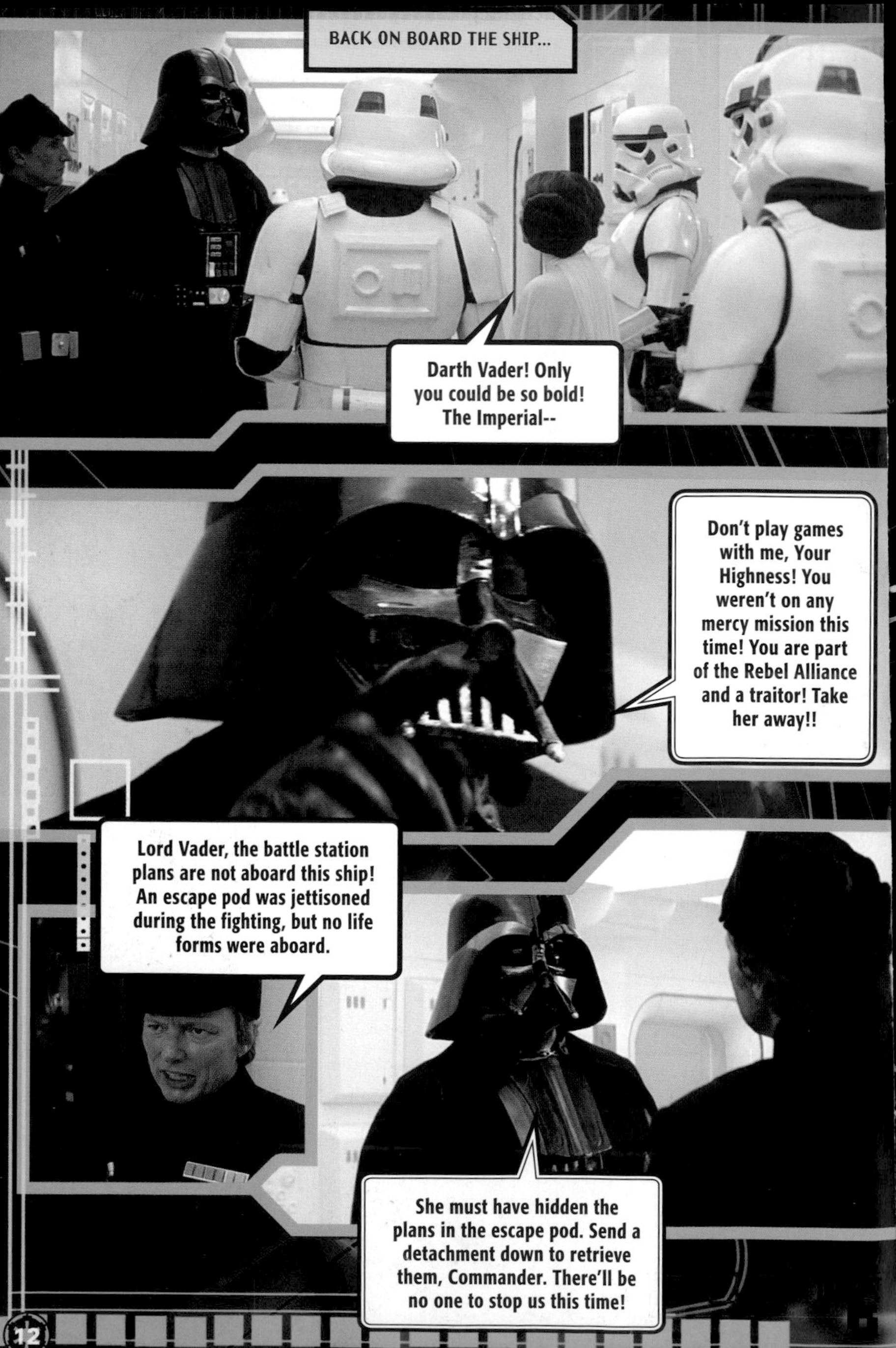
BACK ON BOARD THE SHIP...
Darth Vader! Only you could be so bold! The Imperial--
Don't play games with me, Your Highness! You weren't on any mercy mission this time! You are part of the Rebel Alliance and a traitor! Take her away!!
Lord Vader, the battle station plans are not aboard this ship! An escape pod was jettisoned during the fighting, but no life forms were aboard.
She must have hidden the plans in the escape pod. Send a detachment down to retrieve them, Commander. There'll be no one to stop us this time!

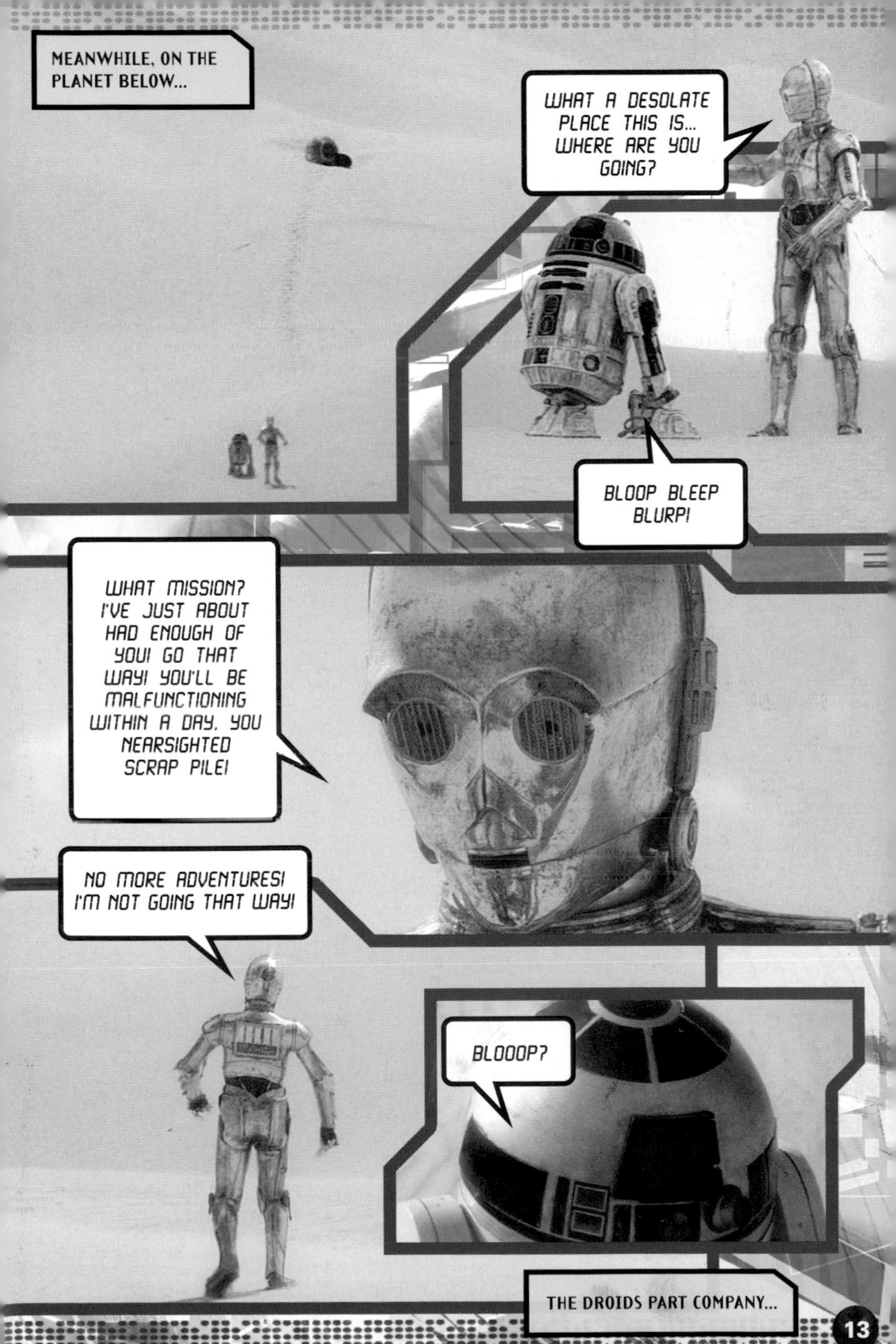
MEANWHILE, ON THE PLANET BELOW...
WHAT A DESOLATE PLACE THIS IS... WHERE ARE YOU GOING?
BLOOP BLEEP BLURP!
WHAT MISSION? I'VE JUST ABOUT HAD ENOUGH OF YOU! GO THAT WAY! YOU'LL BE MALFUNCTIONING WITHIN A DAY, YOU NEARSIGHTED SCRAP PILE!
NO MORE ADVENTURES! I'M NOT GOING THAT WAY!
BLOOOP?
THE DROIDS PART COMPANY...

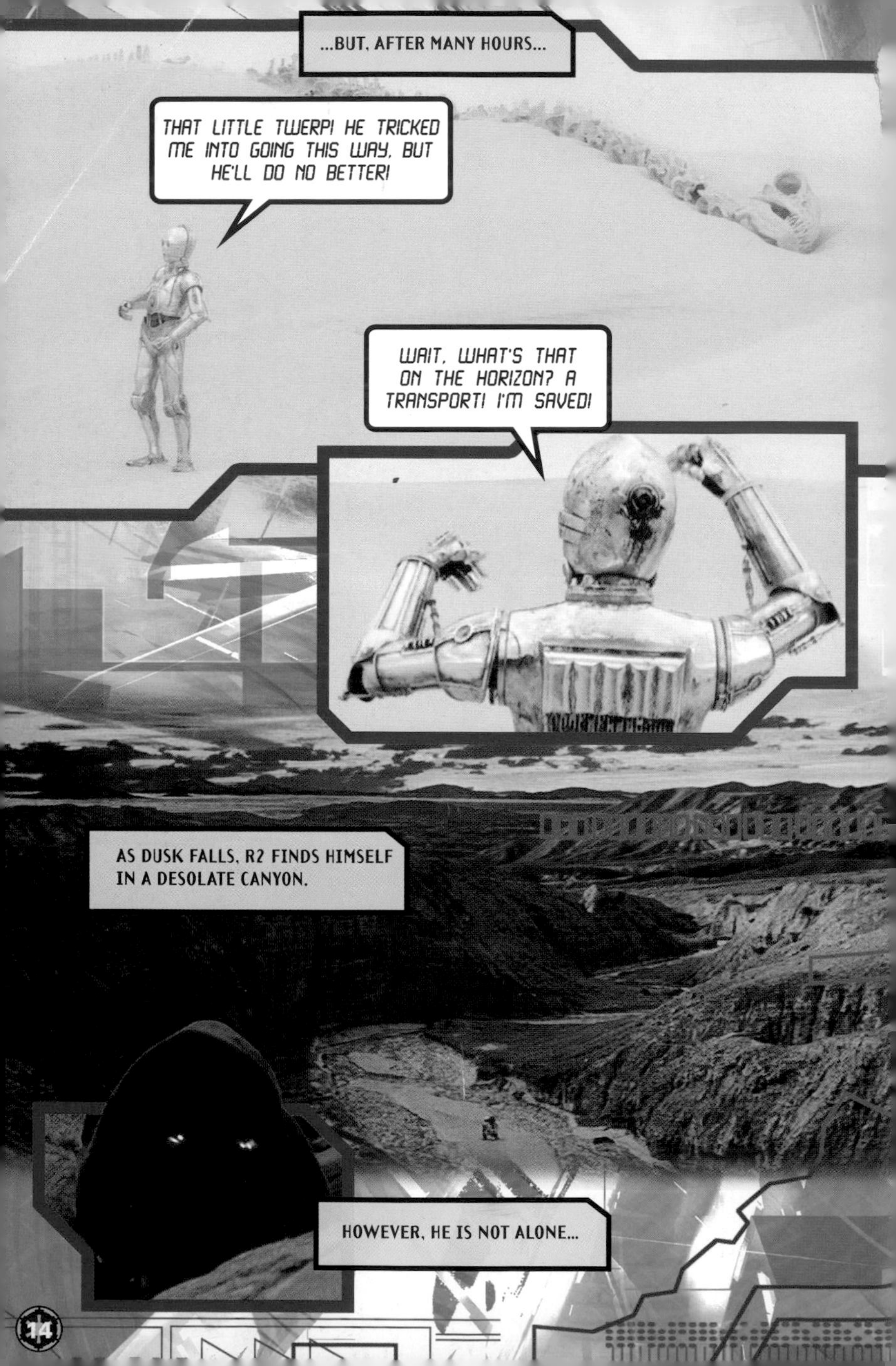

...BUT, AFTER MANY HOURS...
THAT LITTLE TWERP! HE TRICKED ME INTO GOING THIS WAY, BUT HE'LL DO NO BETTER!
WAIT, WHAT'S THAT ON THE HORIZON? A TRANSPORT! I'M SAVED!
AS DUSK FALLS, R2 FINDS HIMSELF IN A DESOLATE CANYON.
HOWEVER, HE IS NOT ALONE...

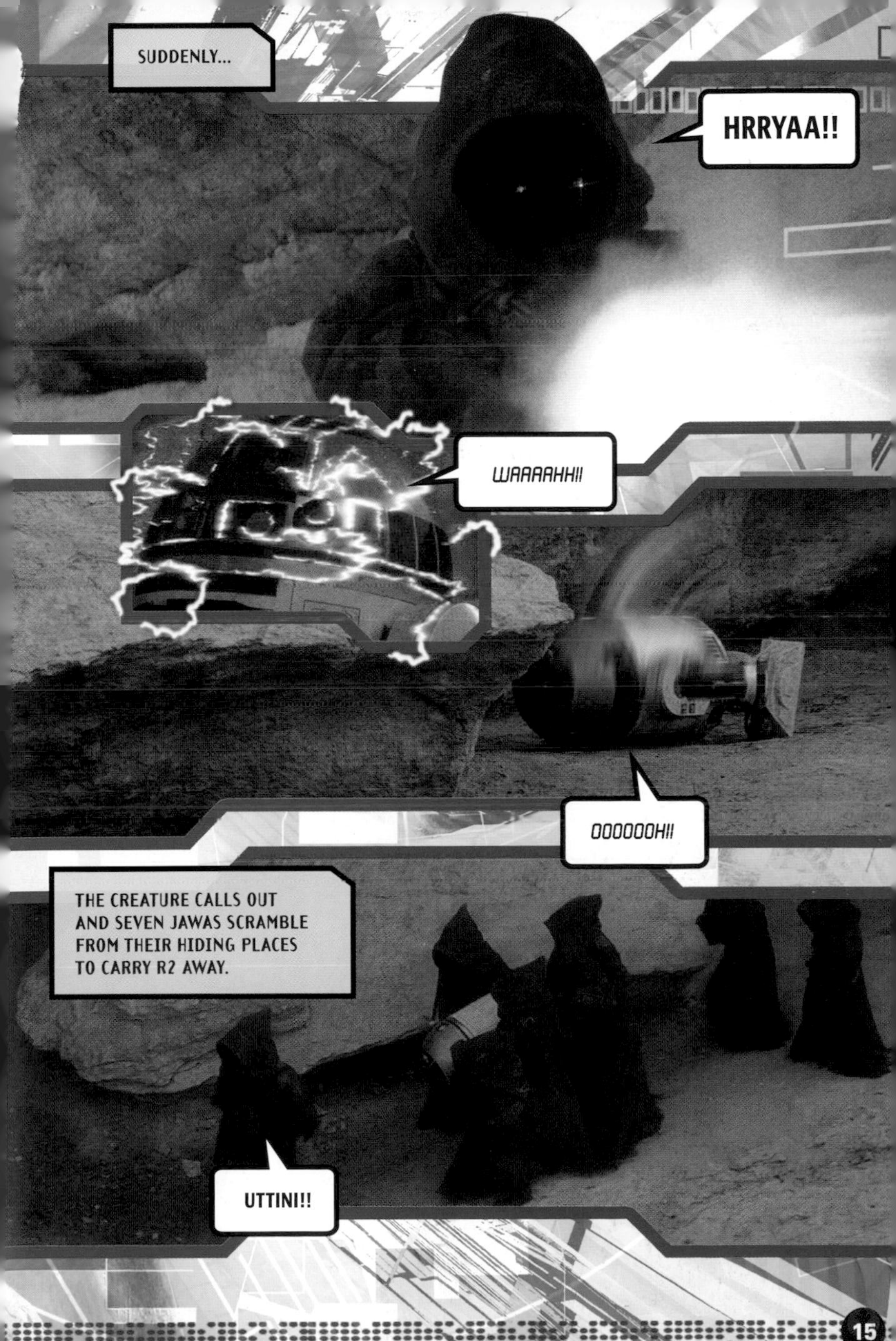
SUDDENLY...
HRRYAA!!
WAAAAHH!!
OOOOOOH!!
THE CREATURE CALLS OUT AND SEVEN JAWAS SCRAMBLE FROM THEIR HIDING PLACES TO CARRY R2 AWAY.
UTTINI!!

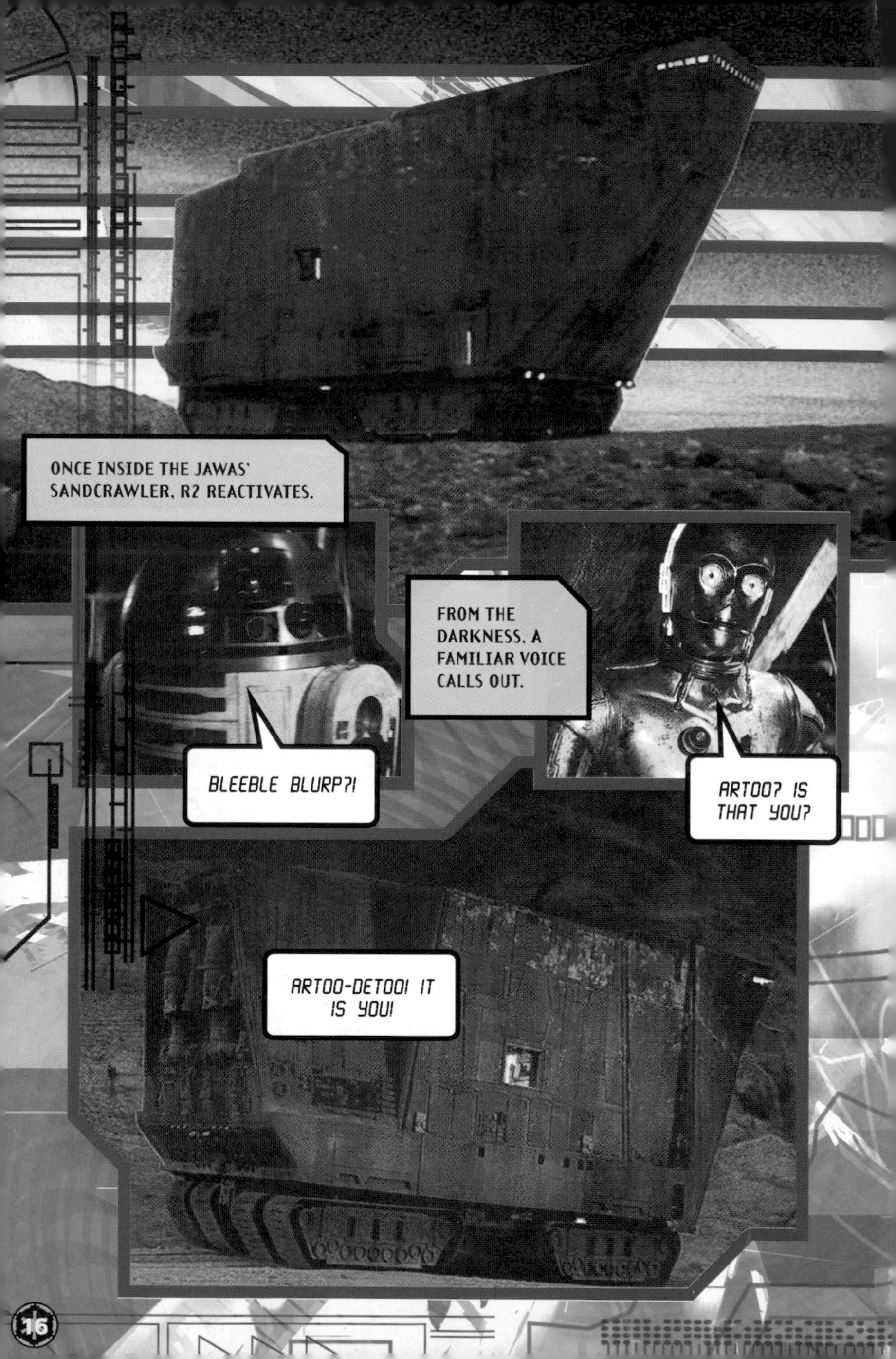

ONCE INSIDE THE JAWAS' SANDCRAWLER, R2 REACTIVATES.
BLEEBLE BLURP?!
FROM THE DARKNESS, A FAMILIAR VOICE CALLS OUT.
ARTOO? IS THAT YOU?
ARTOO-DETOO! IT IS YOU!

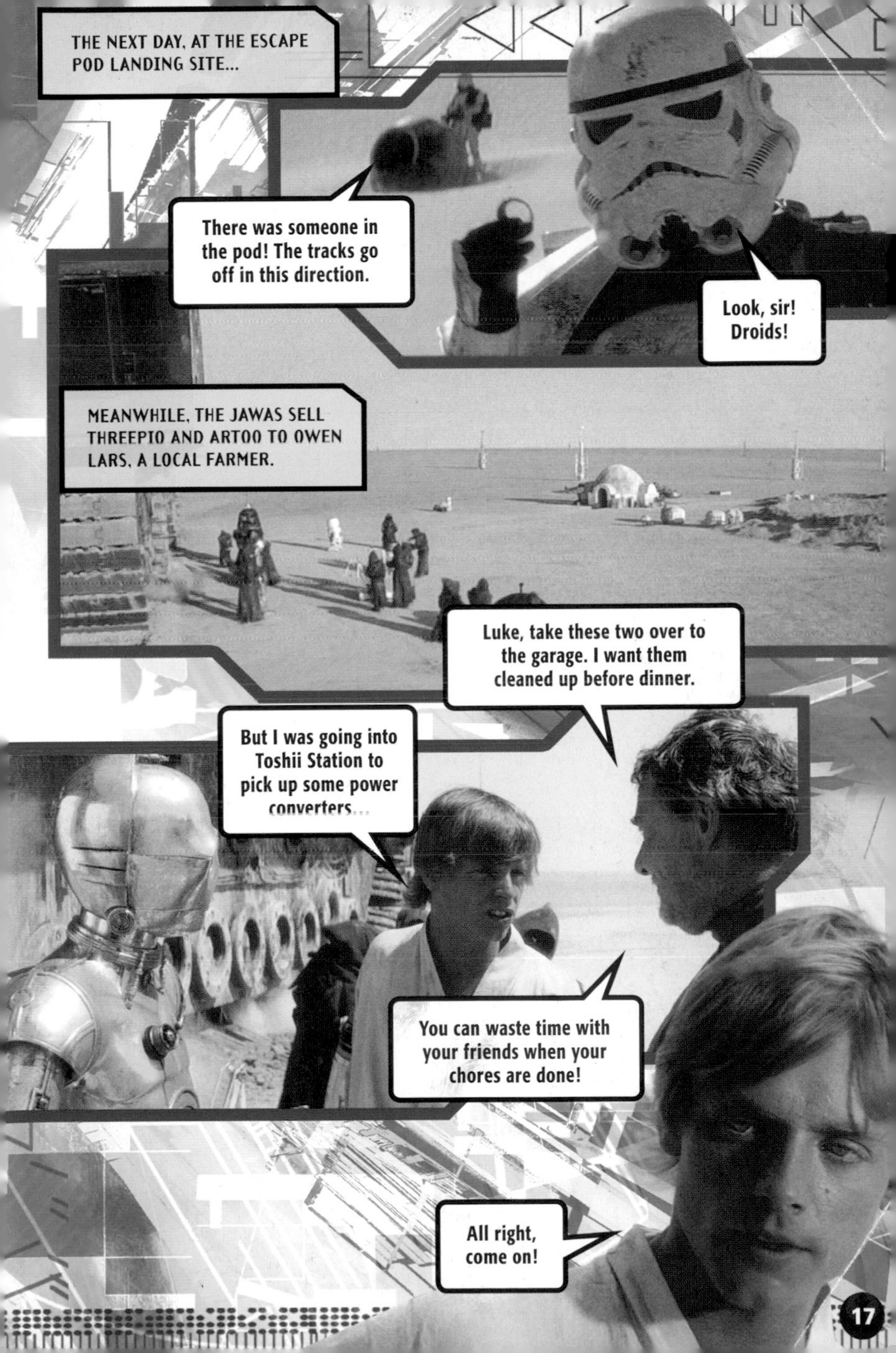
THE NEXT DAY, AT THE ESCAPE POD LANDING SITE...
There was someone in the pod! The tracks go off in this direction.
Look, sir! Droids!
MEANWHILE, THE JAWAS SELL THREEPIO AND ARTOO TO OWEN LARS, A LOCAL FARMER.
Luke, take these two over to the garage. I want them cleaned up before dinner.
But I was going into Toshii Station to pick up some power converters...
You can waste time with your friends when your chores are done!
All right, come on!

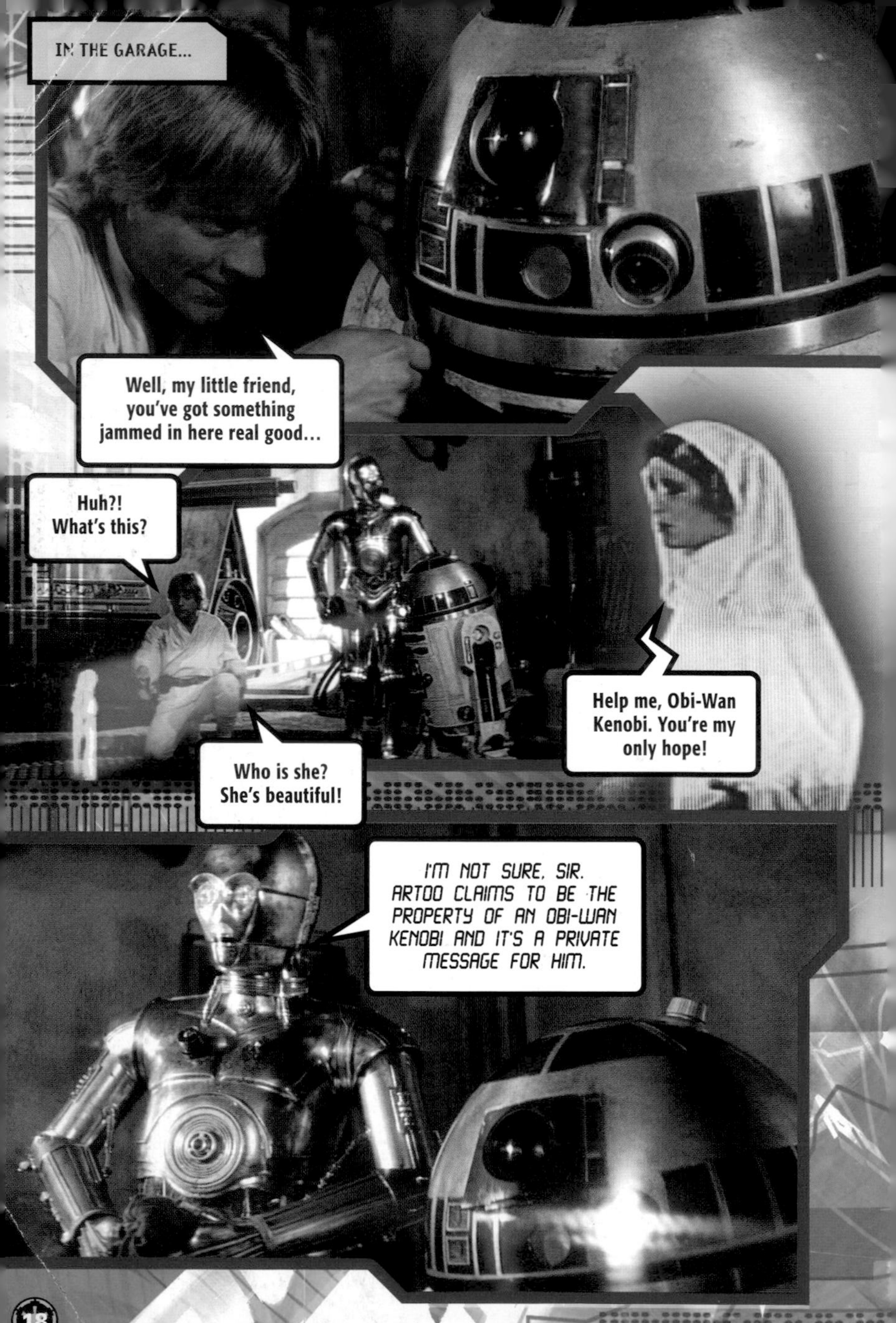
IN THE GARAGE...
Well, my little friend, you've got something jammed in here real good...
Huh?! What's this?
Who is she? She's beautiful!
Help me, Obi-Wan Kenobi. You're my only hope!
I'M NOT SURE, SIR. ARTOO CLAIMS TO BE THE PROPERTY OF AN OBI-WAN KENOBI AND IT'S A PRIVATE MESSAGE FOR HIM.

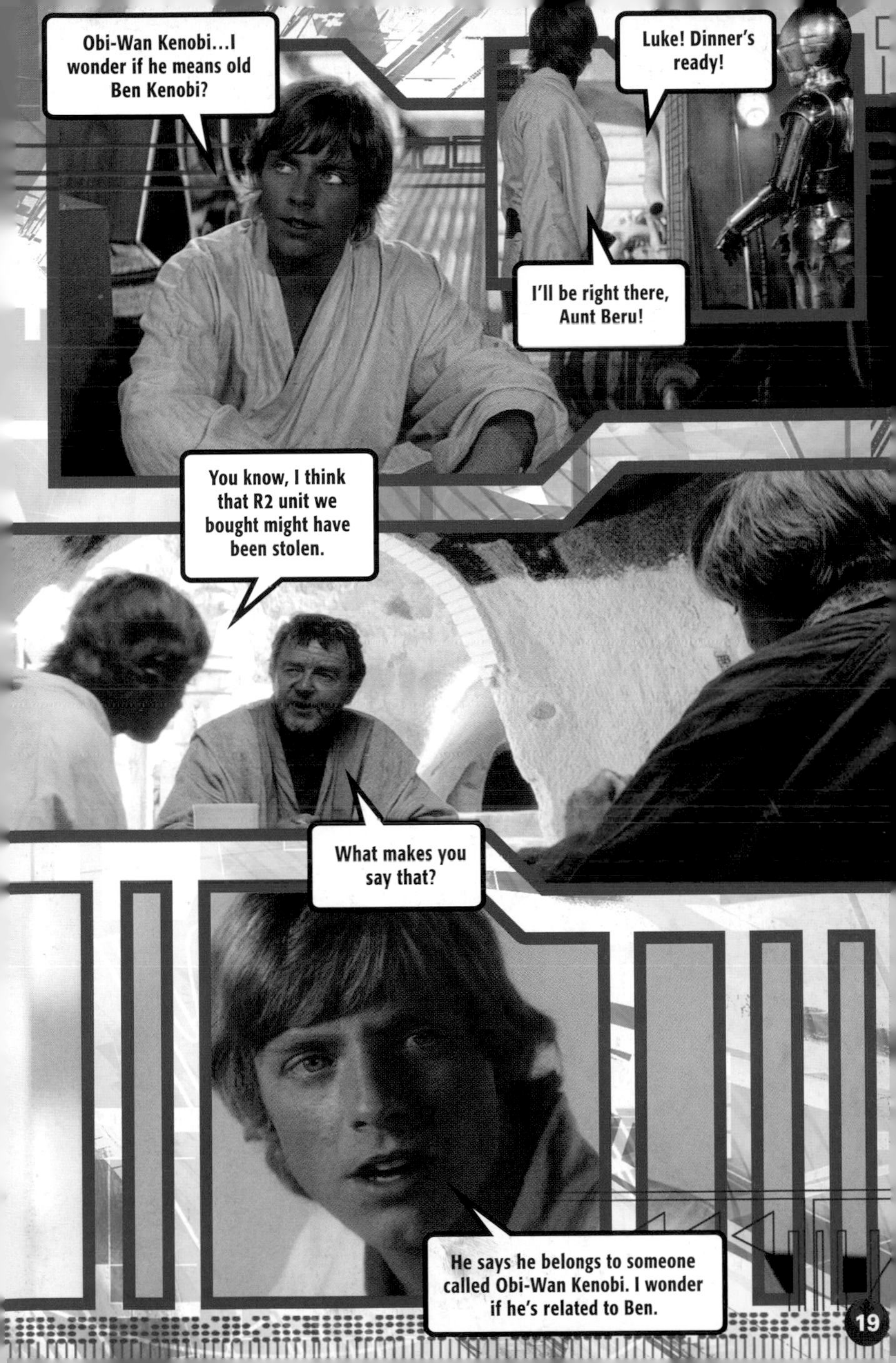
Obi-Wan Kenobi…I wonder if he means old Ben Kenobi?
Luke! Dinner's ready!
I'll be right there, Aunt Beru!
You know, I think that R2 unit we bought might have been stolen.
What makes you say that?
He says he belongs to someone called Obi-Wan Kenobi. I wonder if he's related to Ben.

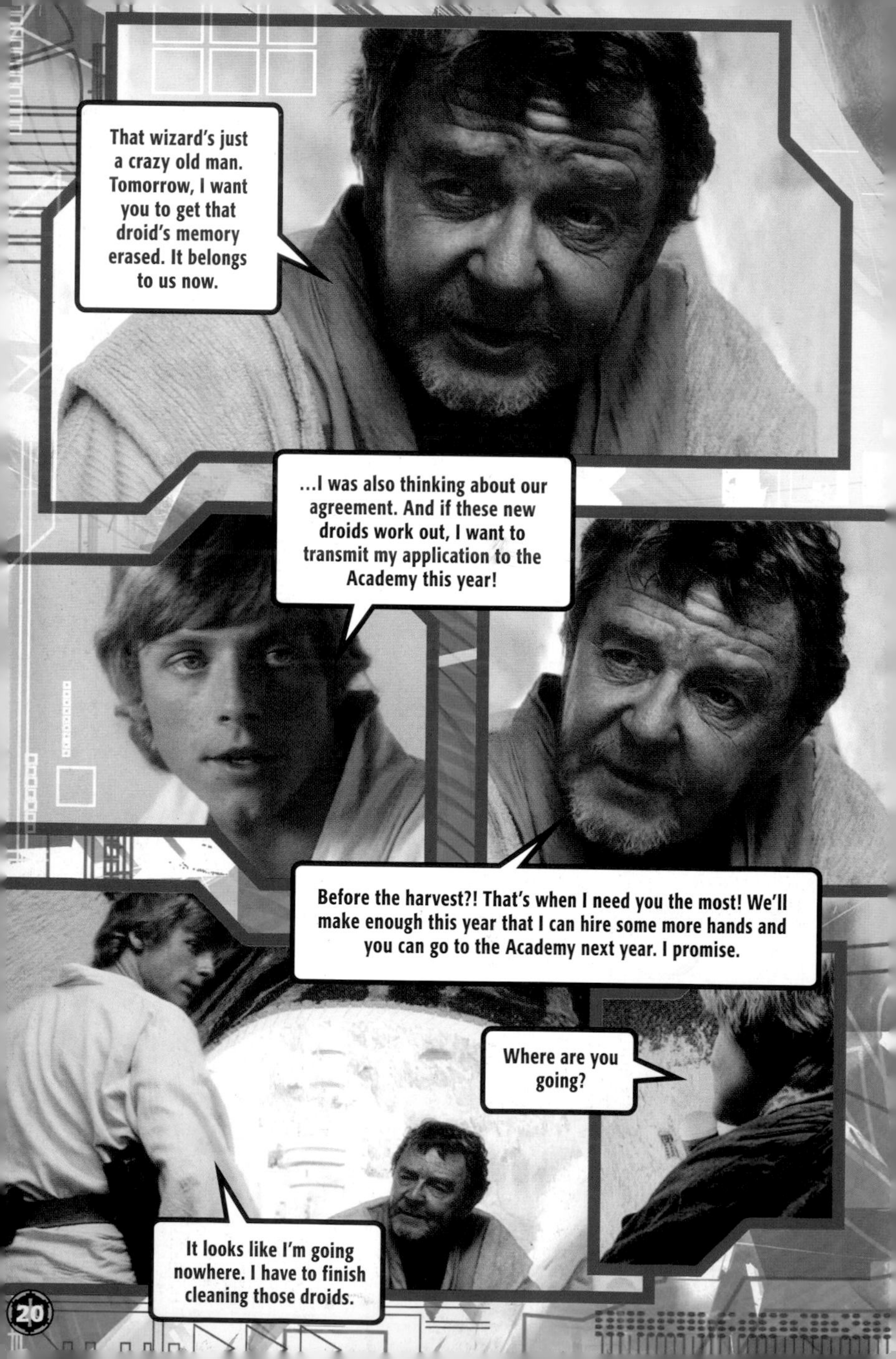
That wizard's just a crazy old man. Tomorrow, I want you to get that droid's memory erased. It belongs to us now.
...I was also thinking about our agreement. And if these new droids work out, I want to transmit my application to the Academy this year!
Before the harvest?! That's when I need you the most! We'll make enough this year that I can hire some more hands and you can go to the Academy next year. I promise.
Where are you going?
It looks like I'm going nowhere. I have to finish cleaning those droids.

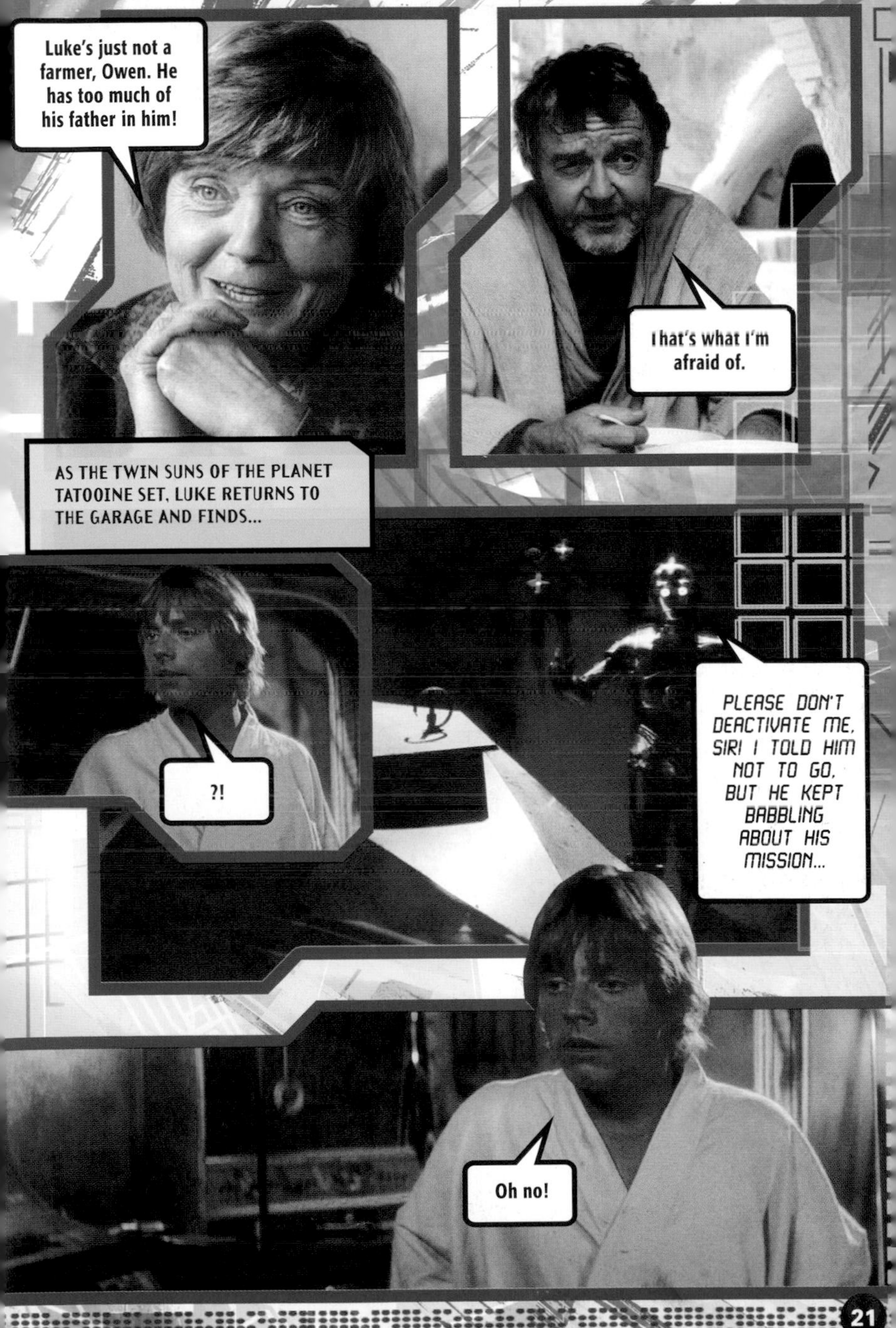
Luke's just not a farmer, Owen. He has too much of his father in him!
That's what I'm afraid of.
AS THE TWIN SUNS OF THE PLANET TATOOINE SET, LUKE RETURNS TO THE GARAGE AND FINDS...
?!
PLEASE DON'T DEACTIVATE ME, SIR! I TOLD HIM NOT TO GO, BUT HE KEPT BABBLING ABOUT HIS MISSION...
Oh no!

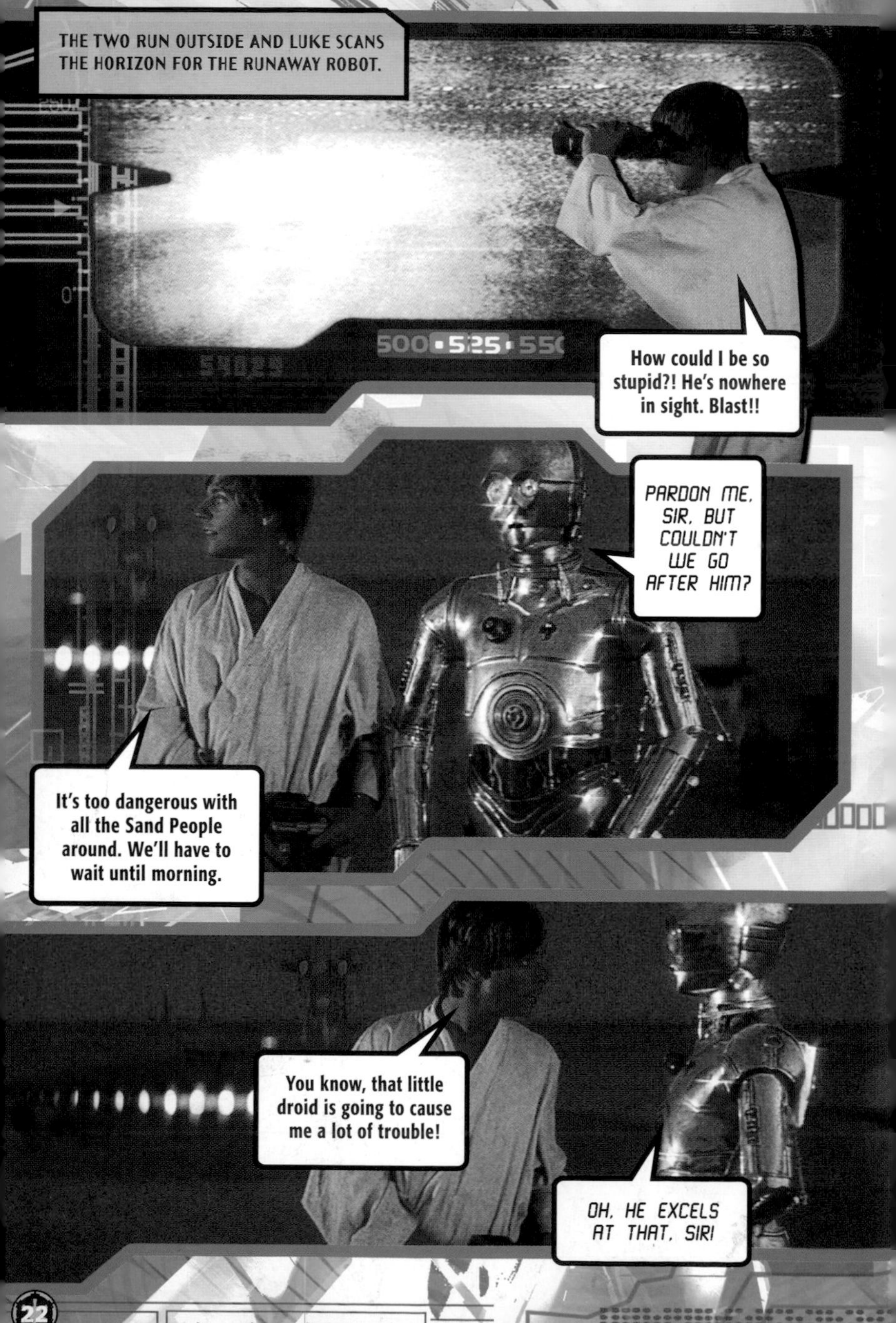
THE TWO RUN OUTSIDE AND LUKE SCANS THE HORIZON FOR THE RUNAWAY ROBOT.
500 • 525 • 550
How could I be so stupid?! He's nowhere in sight. Blast!!
PARDON ME, SIR, BUT COULDN'T WE GO AFTER HIM?
It's too dangerous with all the Sand People around. We'll have to wait until morning.
You know, that little droid is going to cause me a lot of trouble!
OH, HE EXCELS AT THAT, SIR!

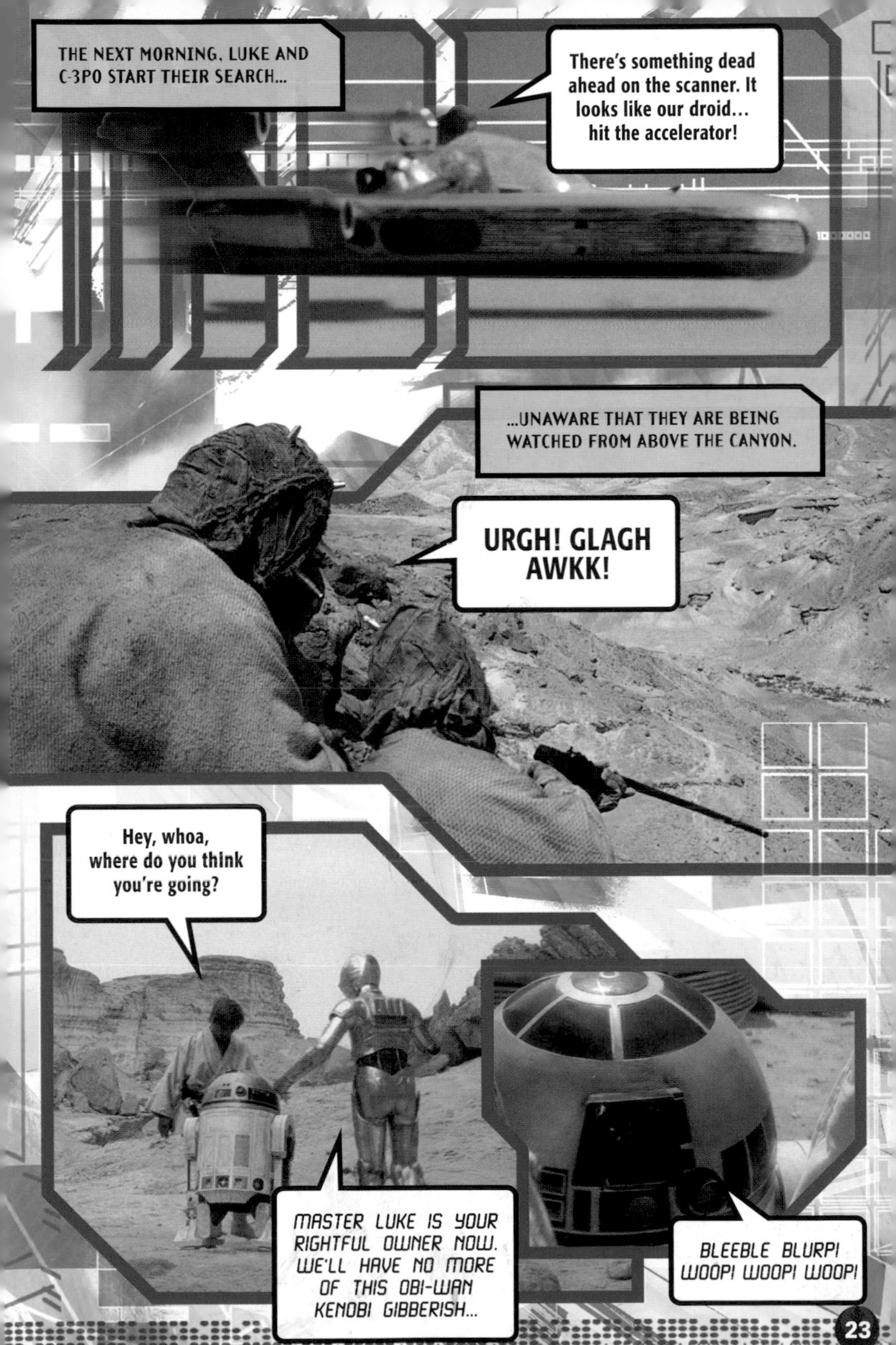
THE NEXT MORNING, LUKE AND C-3PO START THEIR SEARCH...
There's something dead ahead on the scanner. It looks like our droid... hit the accelerator!
...UNAWARE THAT THEY ARE BEING WATCHED FROM ABOVE THE CANYON.
URGH! GLAGH AWKK!
Hey, whoa, where do you think you're going?
MASTER LUKE IS YOUR RIGHTFUL OWNER NOW. WE'LL HAVE NO MORE OF THIS OBI-WAN KENOBI GIBBERISH...
BLEEBLE BLURP! WOOP! WOOP! WOOP!

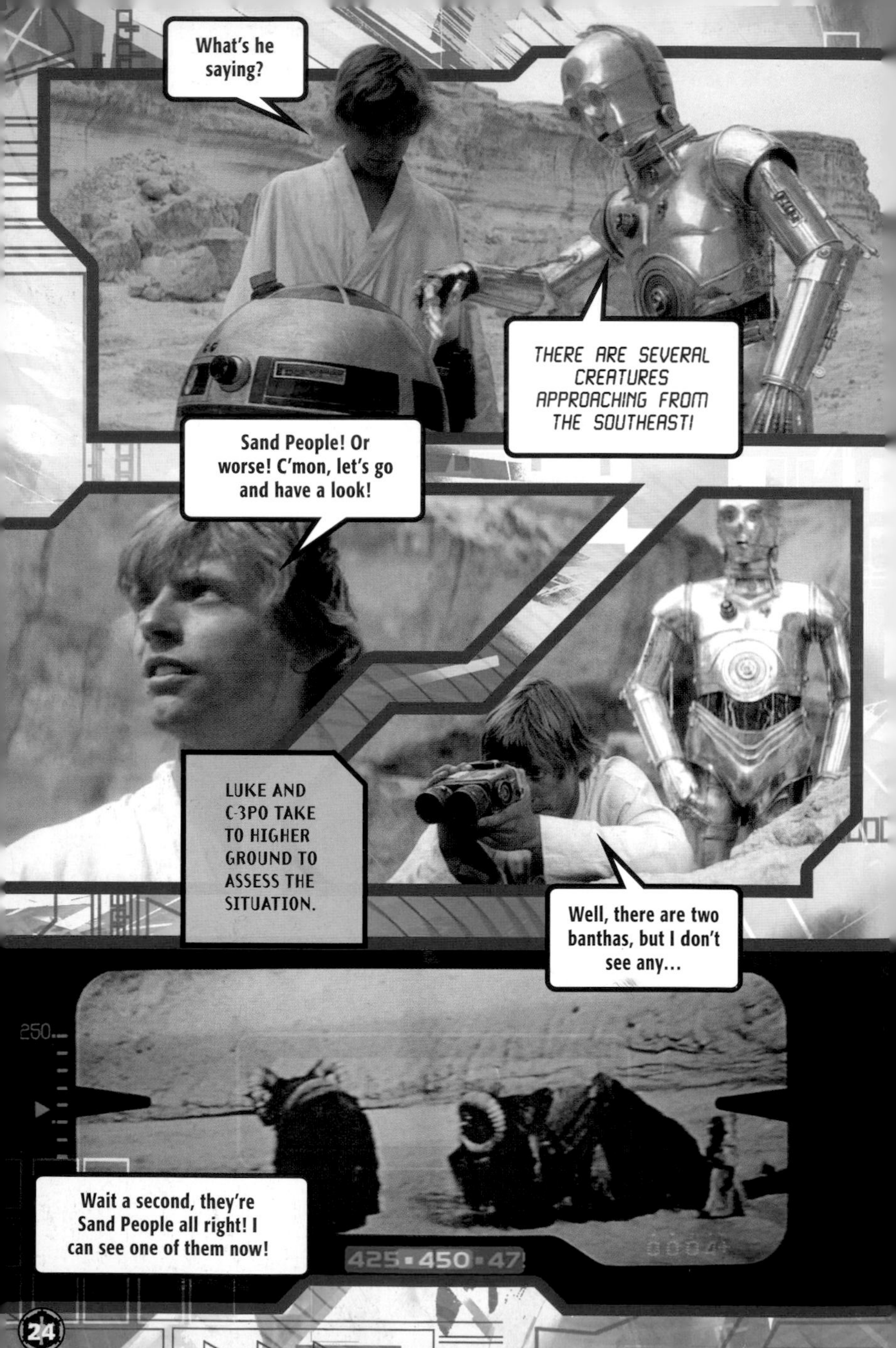
What's he saying?
THERE ARE SEVERAL CREATURES APPROACHING FROM THE SOUTHEAST!
Sand People! Or worse! C'mon, let's go and have a look!
LUKE AND C-3PO TAKE TO HIGHER GROUND TO ASSESS THE SITUATION.
Well, there are two banthas, but I don't see any...
250
425 450 47
Wait a second, they're Sand People all right! I can see one of them now!

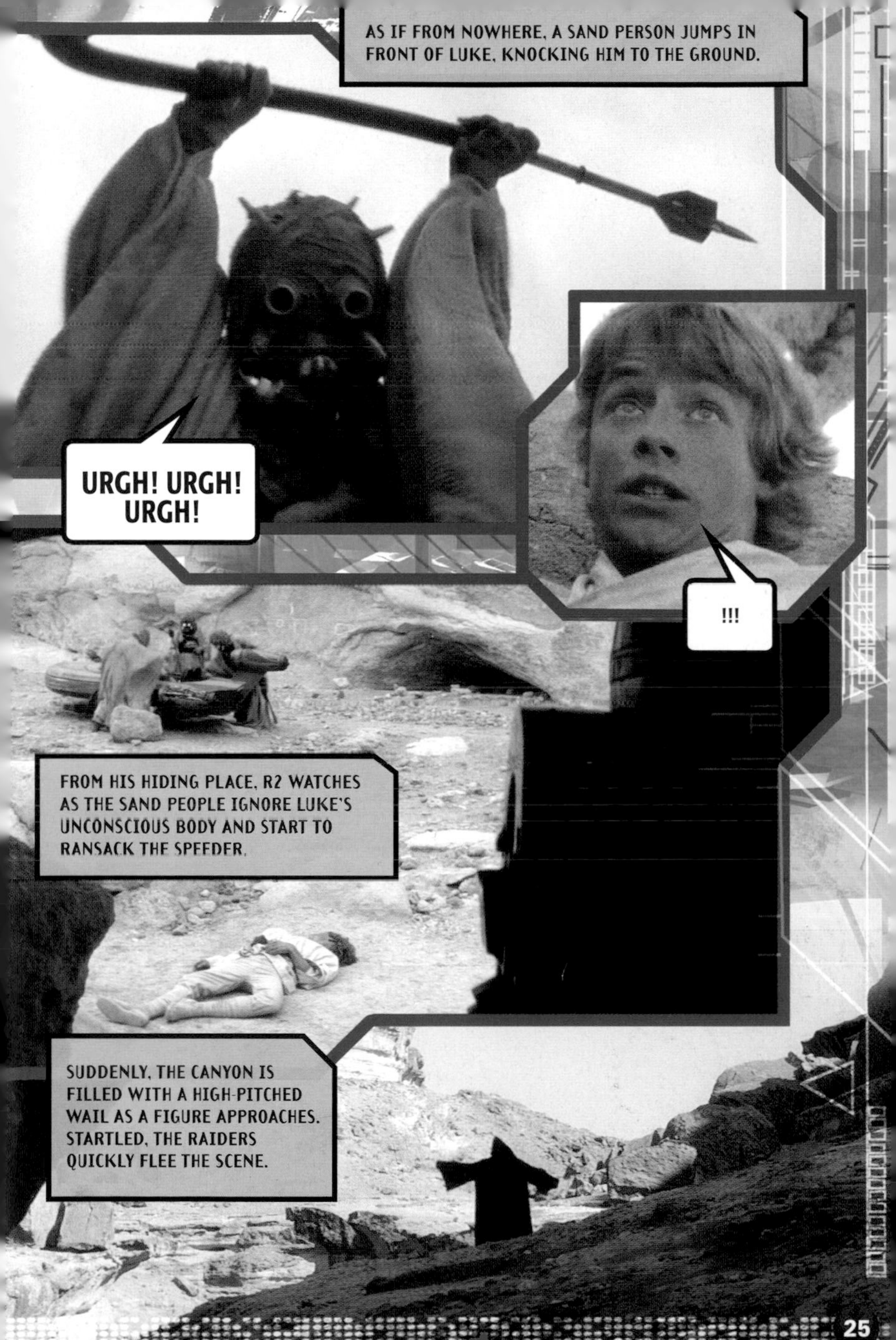
AS IF FROM NOWHERE, A SAND PERSON JUMPS IN FRONT OF LUKE, KNOCKING HIM TO THE GROUND.
URGH! URGH! URGH!
!!!
FROM HIS HIDING PLACE, R2 WATCHES AS THE SAND PEOPLE IGNORE LUKE'S UNCONSCIOUS BODY AND START TO RANSACK THE SPEEDER.
SUDDENLY, THE CANYON IS FILLED WITH A HIGH-PITCHED WAIL AS A FIGURE APPROACHES. STARTLED, THE RAIDERS QUICKLY FLEE THE SCENE.

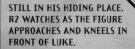

STILL IN HIS HIDING PLACE, R2 WATCHES AS THE FIGURE APPROACHES AND KNEELS IN FRONT OF LUKE.

?!

SLOWLY, LUKE COMES AROUND.

Come here, my little friend. Don't be afraid, he'll be all right!

Ben...Ben Kenobi? Boy, am I glad to see you!

The Jundland Wastes are not to be traveled lightly. Tell me, young Luke, what brings you out this far?

This little droid...

He claims to be the property of an Obi-Wan Kenobi.
SUDDENLY, BEN'S VOICE TAKES A MORE SERIOUS TONE.
Obi-Wan? Now that's a name I haven't heard in a long time...
You know him?!
Well, of course I know him! He's me! But I don't seem to remember ever owning a droid...

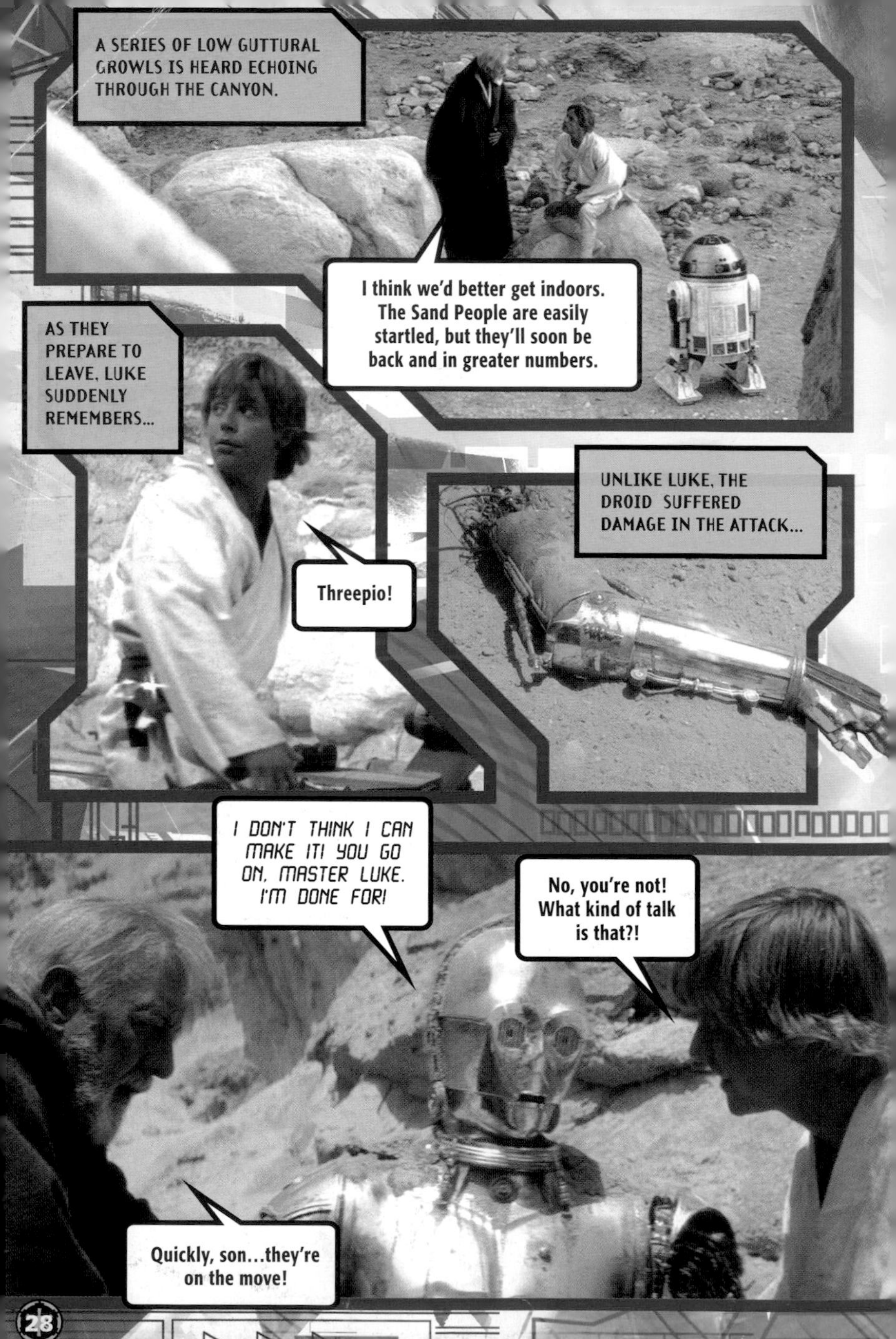

A SERIES OF LOW GUTTURAL GROWLS IS HEARD ECHOING THROUGH THE CANYON.
I think we'd better get indoors. The Sand People are easily startled, but they'll soon be back and in greater numbers.
AS THEY PREPARE TO LEAVE, LUKE SUDDENLY REMEMBERS...
Threepio!
UNLIKE LUKE, THE DROID SUFFERED DAMAGE IN THE ATTACK...
I DON'T THINK I CAN MAKE IT! YOU GO ON, MASTER LUKE. I'M DONE FOR!
No, you're not! What kind of talk is that?!
Quickly, son...they're on the move!

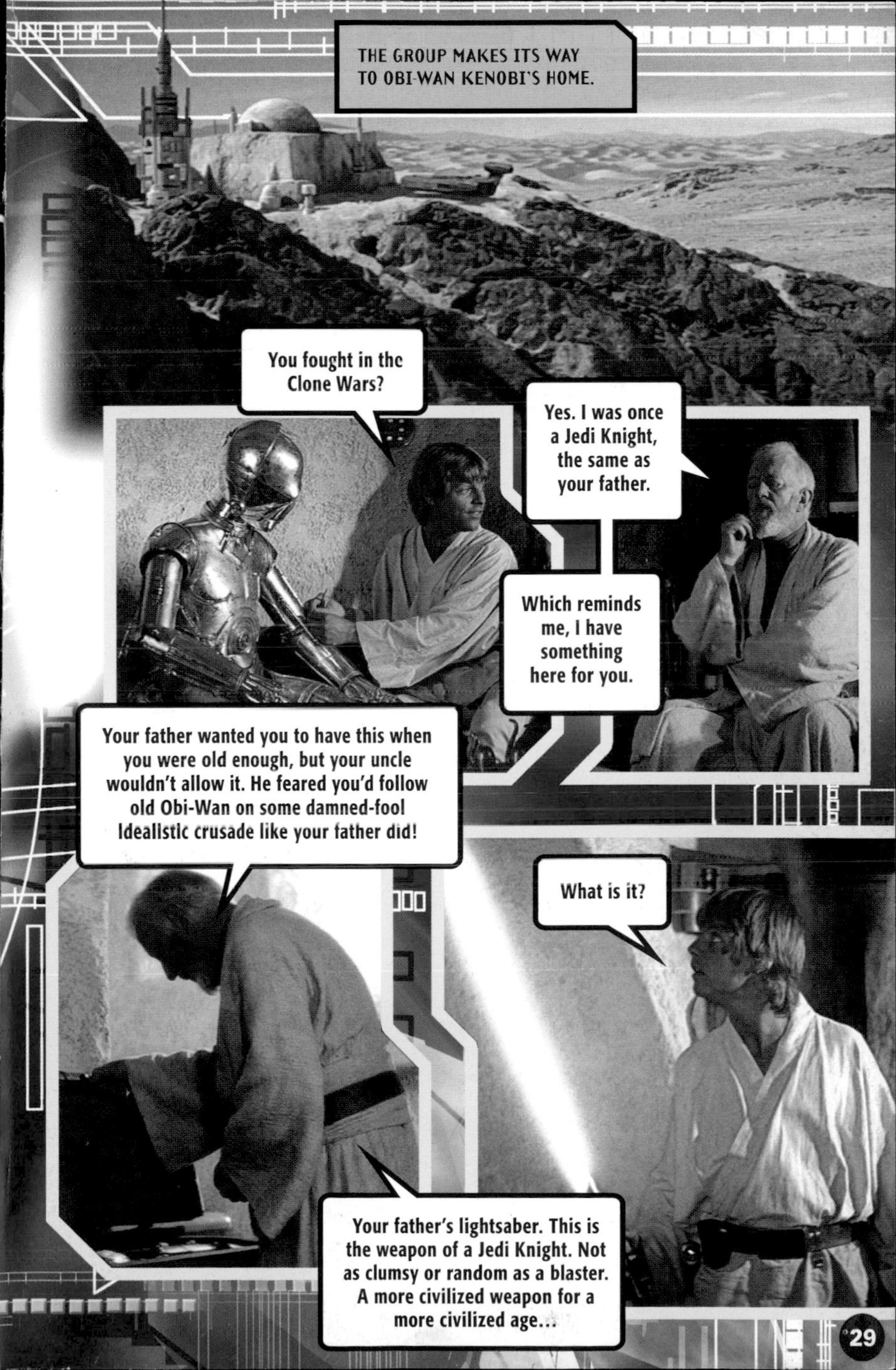
THE GROUP MAKES ITS WAY TO OBI-WAN KENOBI'S HOME.
You fought in the Clone Wars?
Yes. I was once a Jedi Knight, the same as your father.
Which reminds me, I have something here for you.
Your father wanted you to have this when you were old enough, but your uncle wouldn't allow it. He feared you'd follow old Obi-Wan on some damned-fool idealistic crusade like your father did!
What is it?
Your father's lightsaber. This is the weapon of a Jedi Knight. Not as clumsy or random as a blaster. A more civilized weapon for a more civilized age...

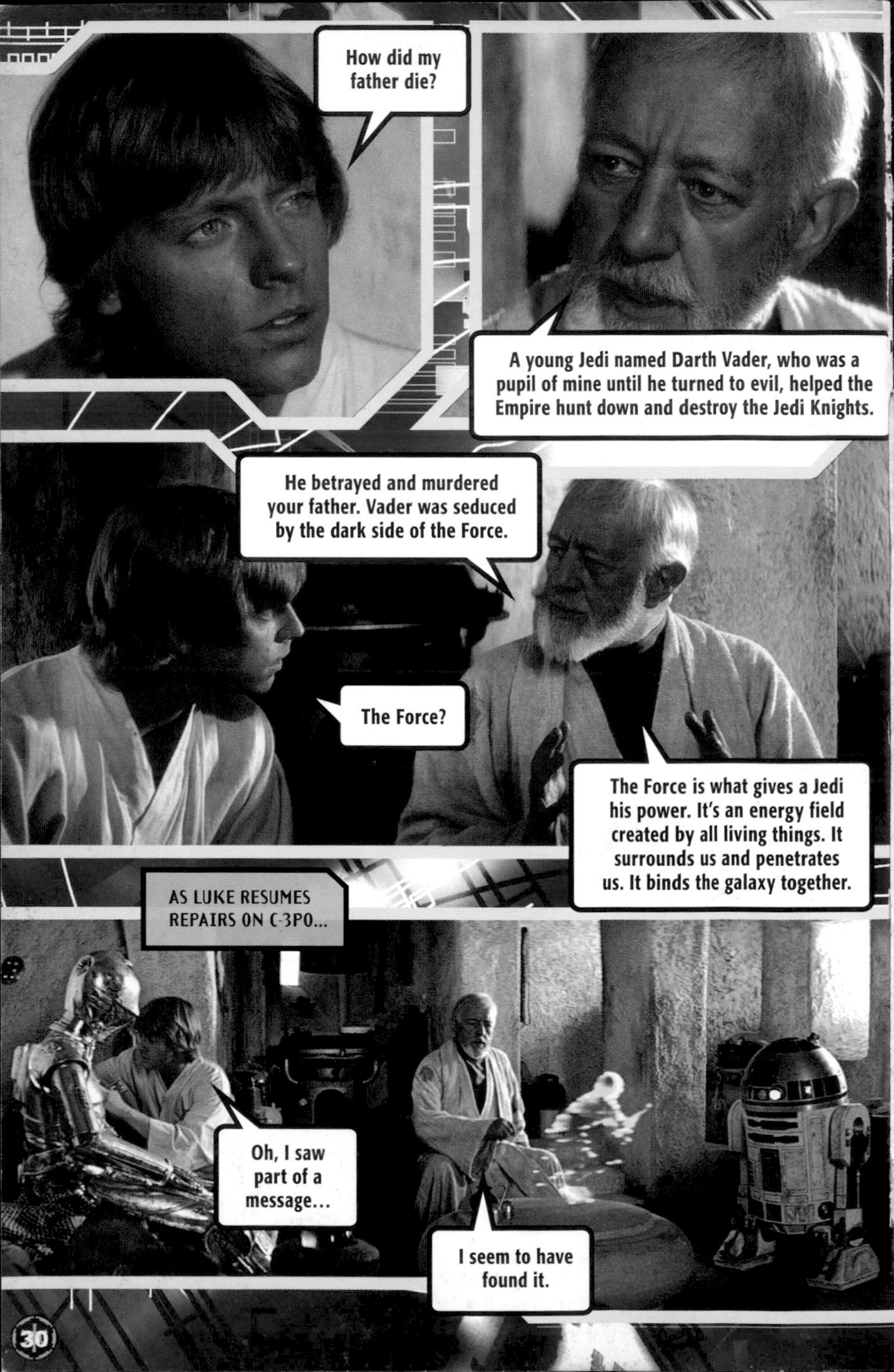
How did my father die?
A young Jedi named Darth Vader, who was a pupil of mine until he turned to evil, helped the Empire hunt down and destroy the Jedi Knights.
He betrayed and murdered your father. Vader was seduced by the dark side of the Force.
The Force?
The Force is what gives a Jedi his power. It's an energy field created by all living things. It surrounds us and penetrates us. It binds the galaxy together.
AS LUKE RESUMES REPAIRS ON C-3PO...
Oh, I saw part of a message...
I seem to have found it.

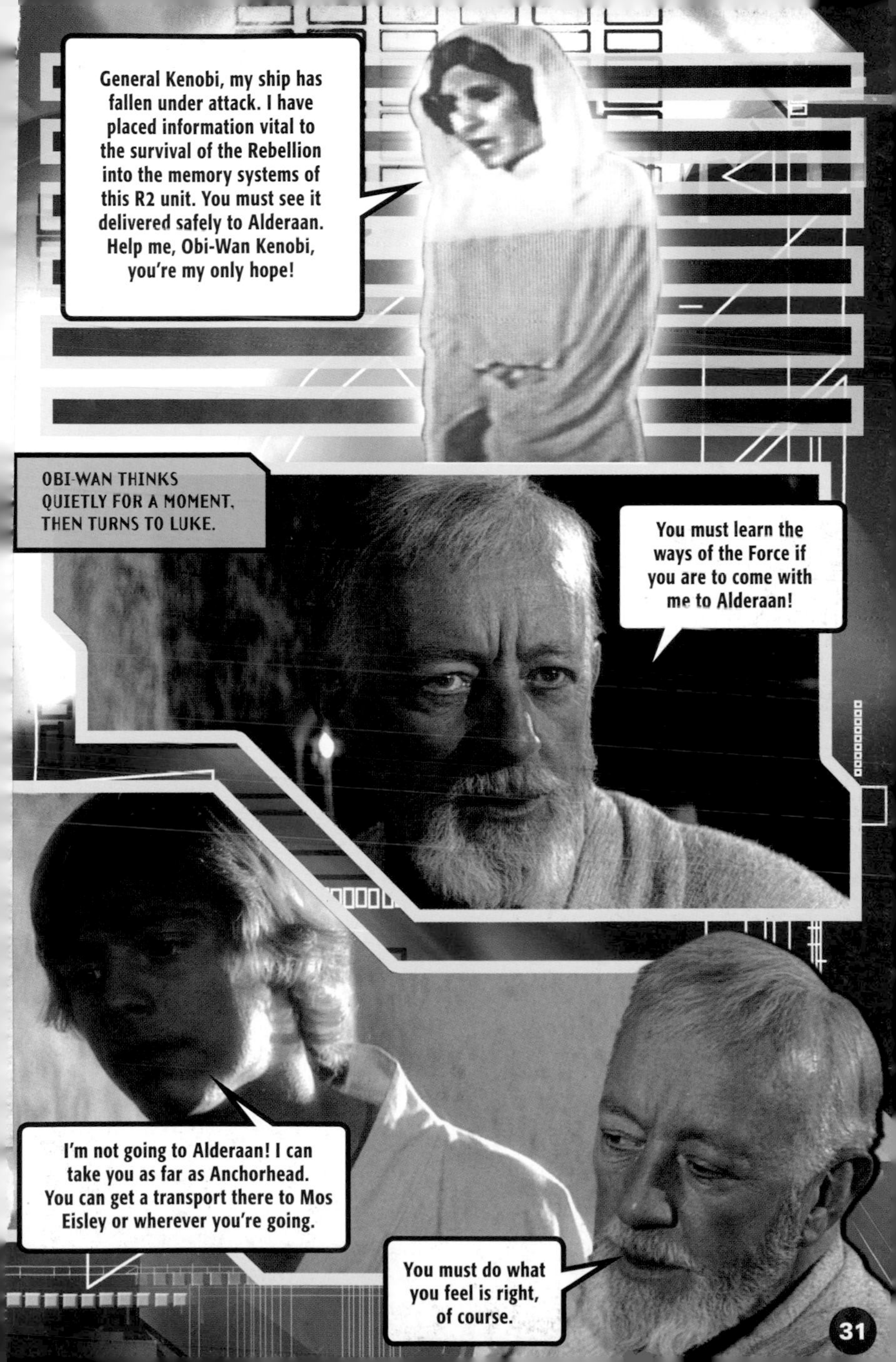
General Kenobi, my ship has fallen under attack. I have placed information vital to the survival of the Rebellion into the memory systems of this R2 unit. You must see it delivered safely to Alderaan. Help me, Obi-Wan Kenobi, you're my only hope!
OBI-WAN THINKS QUIETLY FOR A MOMENT, THEN TURNS TO LUKE.
You must learn the ways of the Force if you are to come with me to Alderaan!
I'm not going to Alderaan! I can take you as far as Anchorhead. You can get a transport there to Mos Eisley or wherever you're going.
You must do what you feel is right, of course.

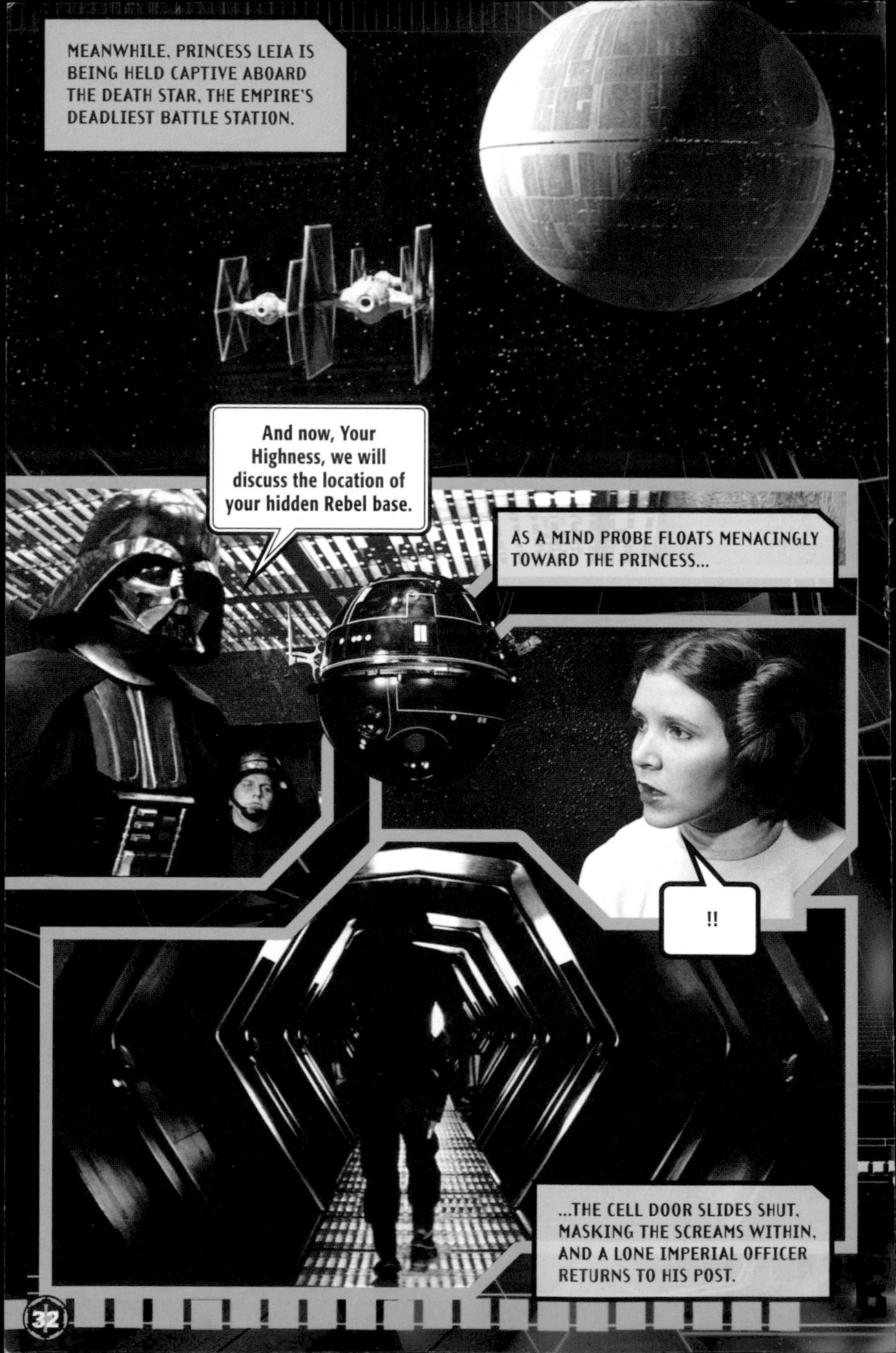
MEANWHILE, PRINCESS LEIA IS BEING HELD CAPTIVE ABOARD THE DEATH STAR, THE EMPIRE'S DEADLIEST BATTLE STATION.
And now, Your Highness, we will discuss the location of your hidden Rebel base.
AS A MIND PROBE FLOATS MENACINGLY TOWARD THE PRINCESS...
!!
...THE CELL DOOR SLIDES SHUT, MASKING THE SCREAMS WITHIN, AND A LONE IMPERIAL OFFICER RETURNS TO HIS POST.

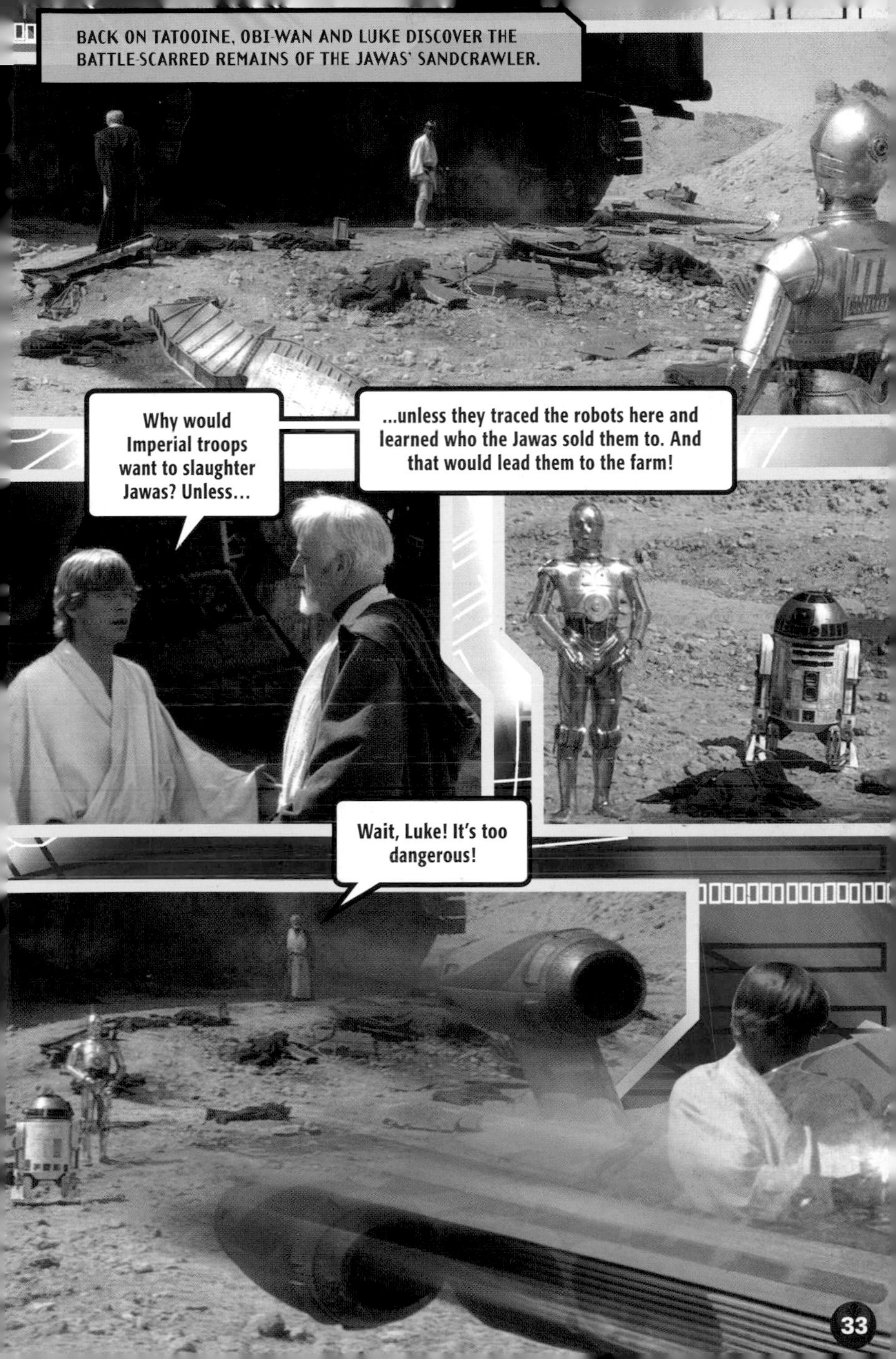
BACK ON TATOOINE, OBI-WAN AND LUKE DISCOVER THE BATTLE-SCARRED REMAINS OF THE JAWAS' SANDCRAWLER.
Why would Imperial troops want to slaughter Jawas? Unless...
...unless they traced the robots here and learned who the Jawas sold them to. And that would lead them to the farm!
Wait, Luke! It's too dangerous!

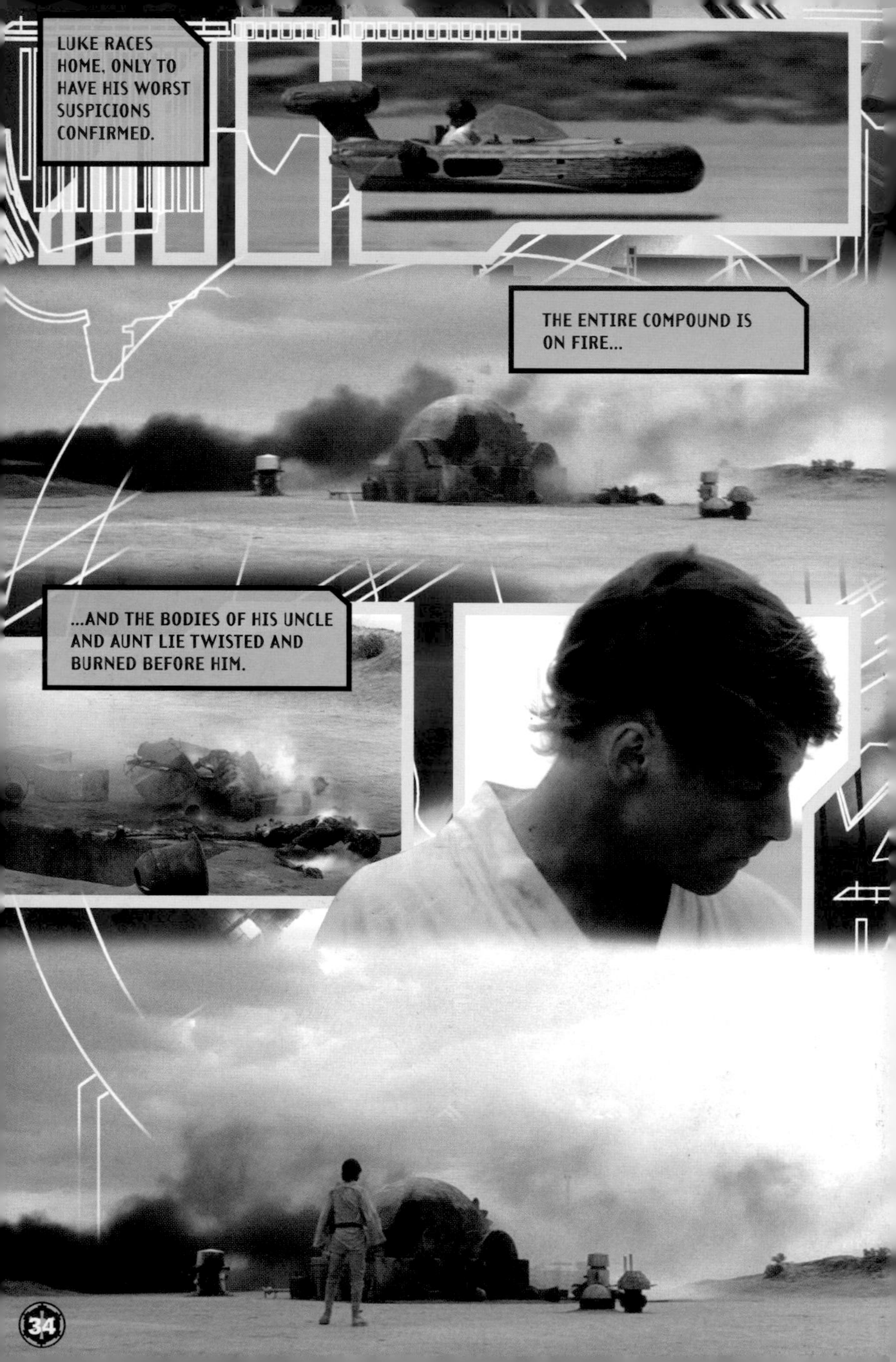
LUKE RACES HOME, ONLY TO HAVE HIS WORST SUSPICIONS CONFIRMED.
THE ENTIRE COMPOUND IS ON FIRE...
...AND THE BODIES OF HIS UNCLE AND AUNT LIE TWISTED AND BURNED BEFORE HIM.

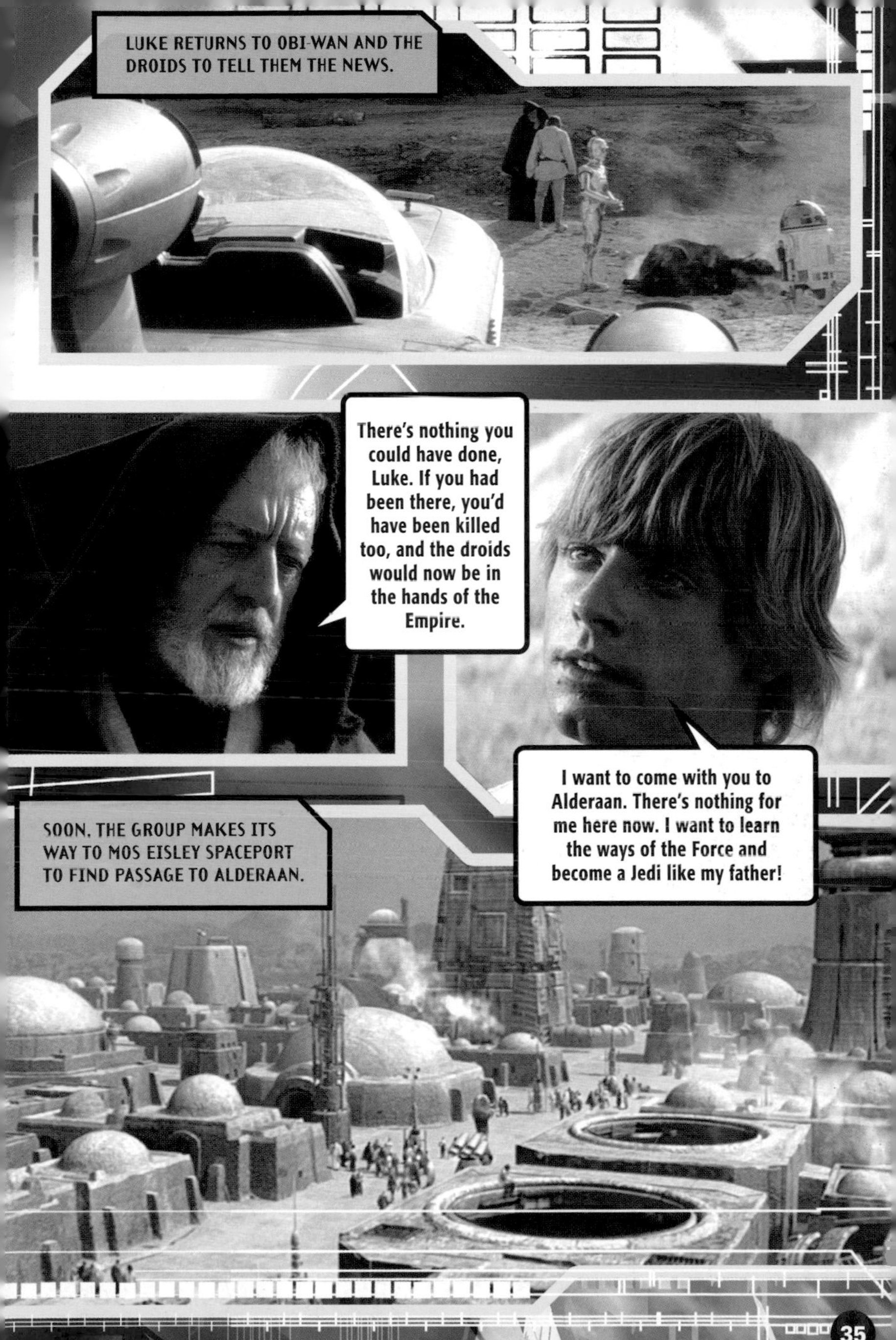
LUKE RETURNS TO OBI-WAN AND THE DROIDS TO TELL THEM THE NEWS.
There's nothing you could have done, Luke. If you had been there, you'd have been killed too, and the droids would now be in the hands of the Empire.
I want to come with you to Alderaan. There's nothing for me here now. I want to learn the ways of the Force and become a Jedi like my father!
SOON, THE GROUP MAKES ITS WAY TO MOS EISLEY SPACEPORT TO FIND PASSAGE TO ALDERAAN.

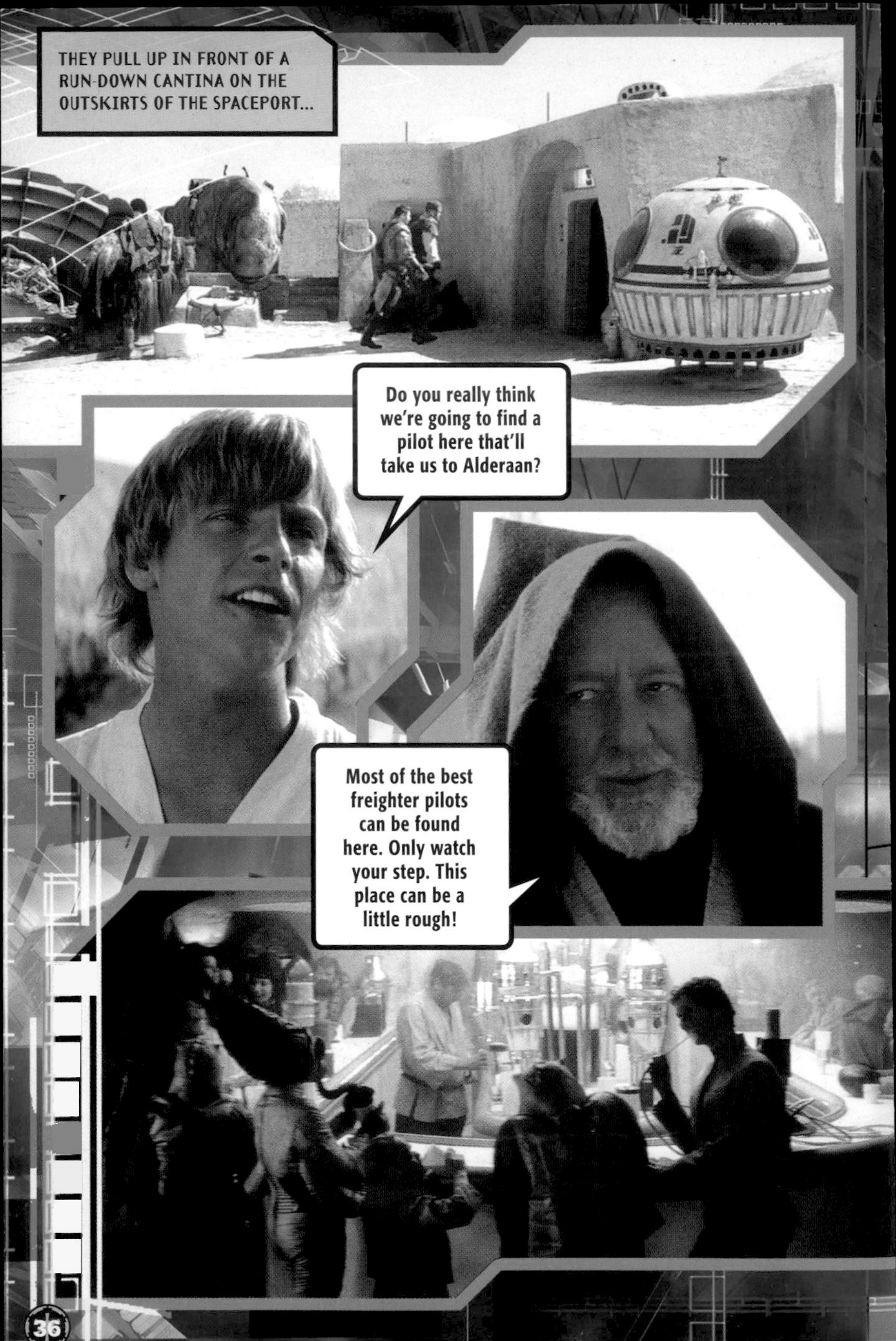

THEY PULL UP IN FRONT OF A RUN-DOWN CANTINA ON THE OUTSKIRTS OF THE SPACEPORT...
Do you really think we're going to find a pilot here that'll take us to Alderaan?
Most of the best freighter pilots can be found here. Only watch your step. This place can be a little rough!

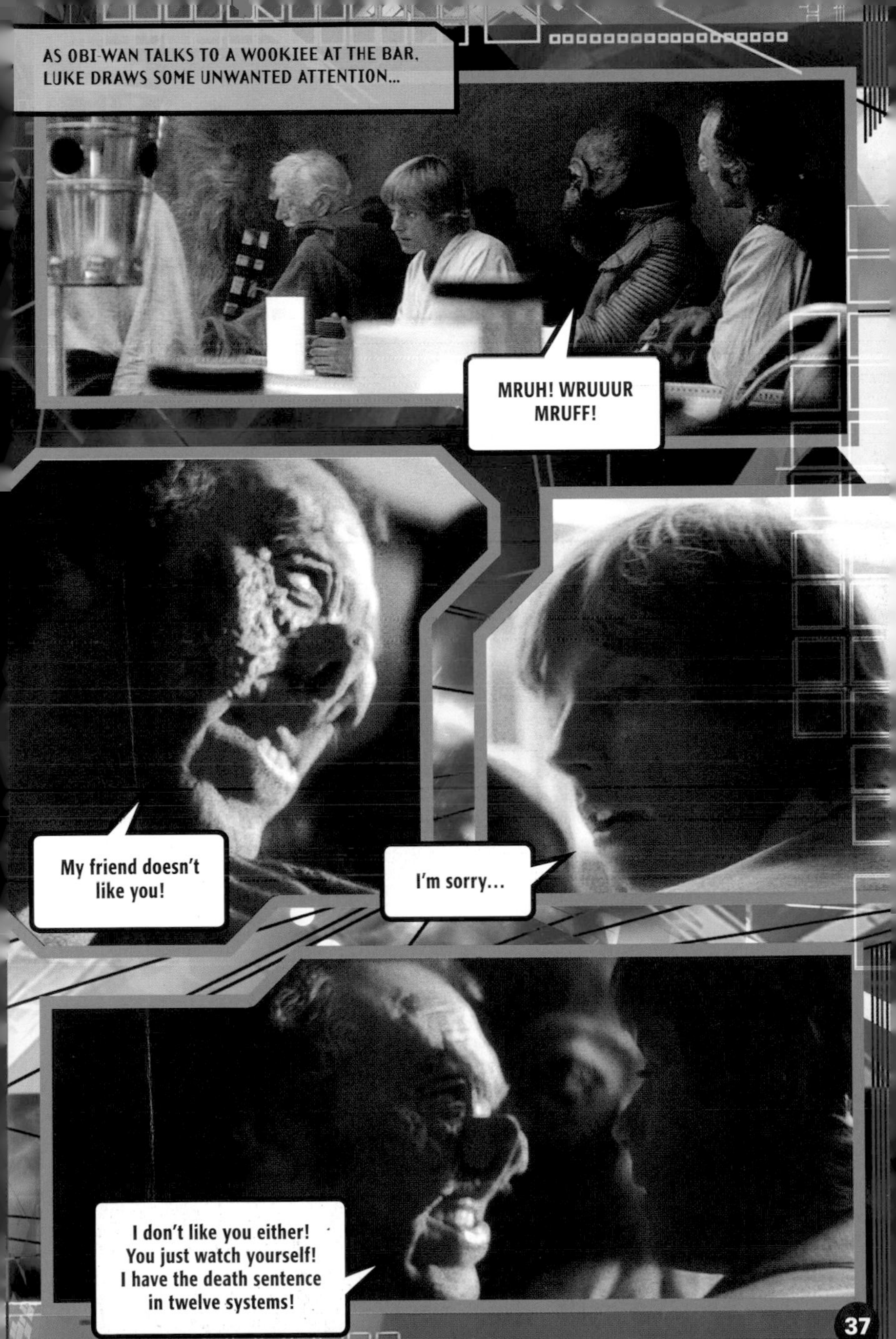

AS OBI-WAN TALKS TO A WOOKIEE AT THE BAR, LUKE DRAWS SOME UNWANTED ATTENTION...
MRUH! WRUUUR MRUFF!
My friend doesn't like you!
I'm sorry...
I don't like you either! You just watch yourself! I have the death sentence in twelve systems!

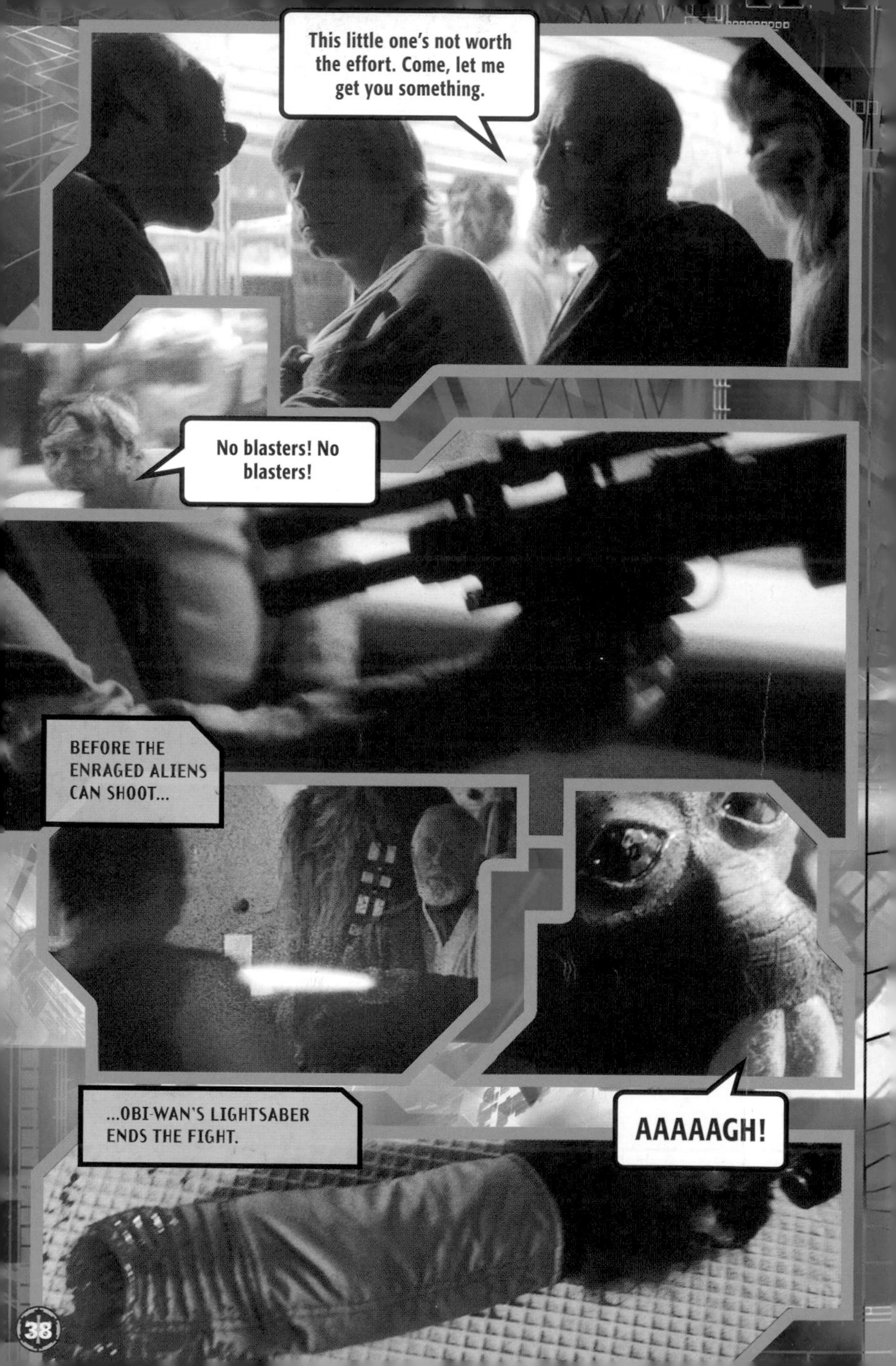
This little one's not worth the effort. Come, let me get you something.
No blasters! No blasters!
BEFORE THE ENRAGED ALIENS CAN SHOOT...
...OBI-WAN'S LIGHTSABER ENDS THE FIGHT.
AAAAAGH!

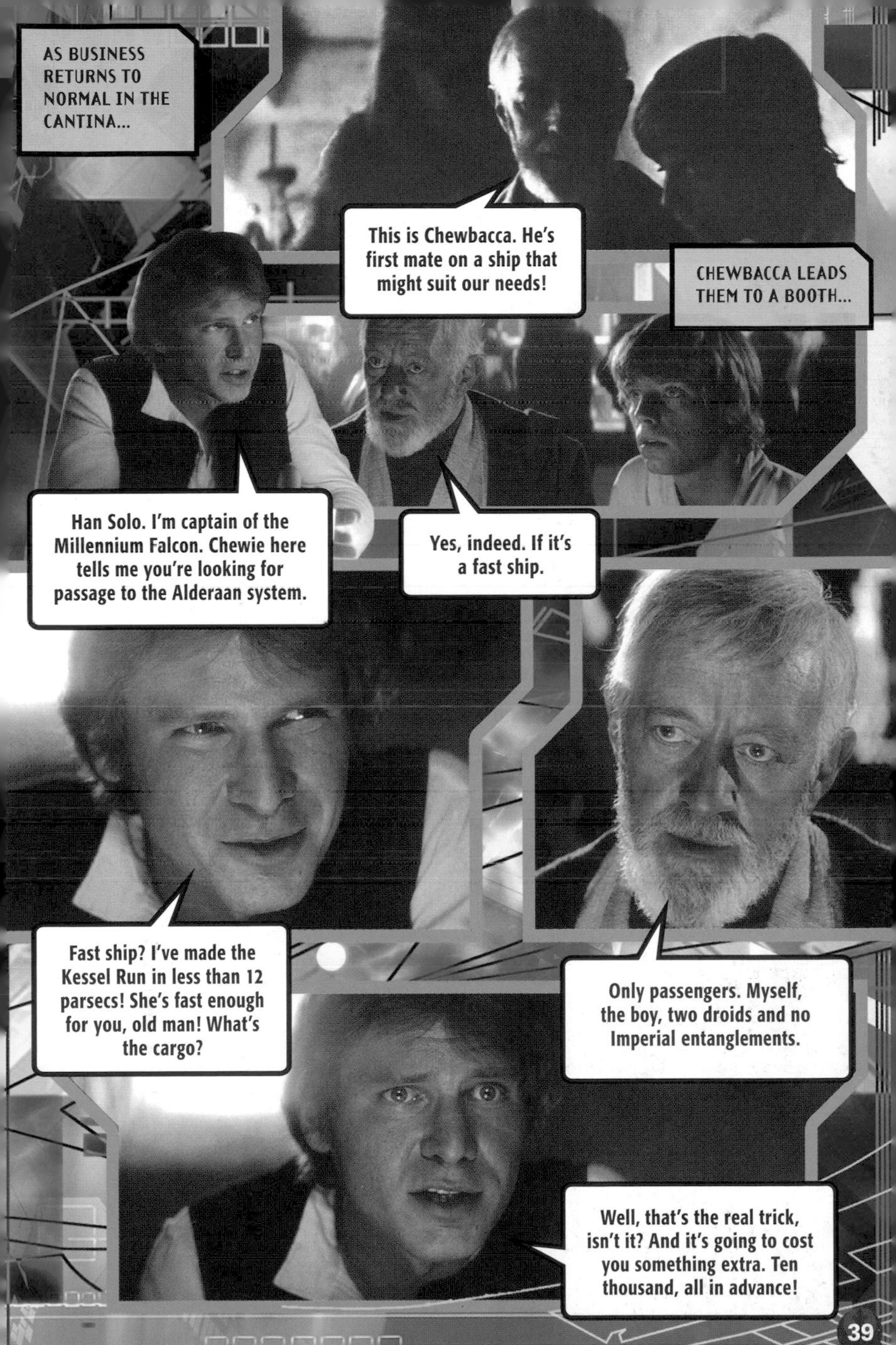
AS BUSINESS RETURNS TO NORMAL IN THE CANTINA...
This is Chewbacca. He's first mate on a ship that might suit our needs!
CHEWBACCA LEADS THEM TO A BOOTH...
Han Solo. I'm captain of the Millennium Falcon. Chewie here tells me you're looking for passage to the Alderaan system.
Yes, indeed. If it's a fast ship.
Fast ship? I've made the Kessel Run in less than 12 parsecs! She's fast enough for you, old man! What's the cargo?
Only passengers. Myself, the boy, two droids and no Imperial entanglements.
Well, that's the real trick, isn't it? And it's going to cost you something extra. Ten thousand, all in advance!

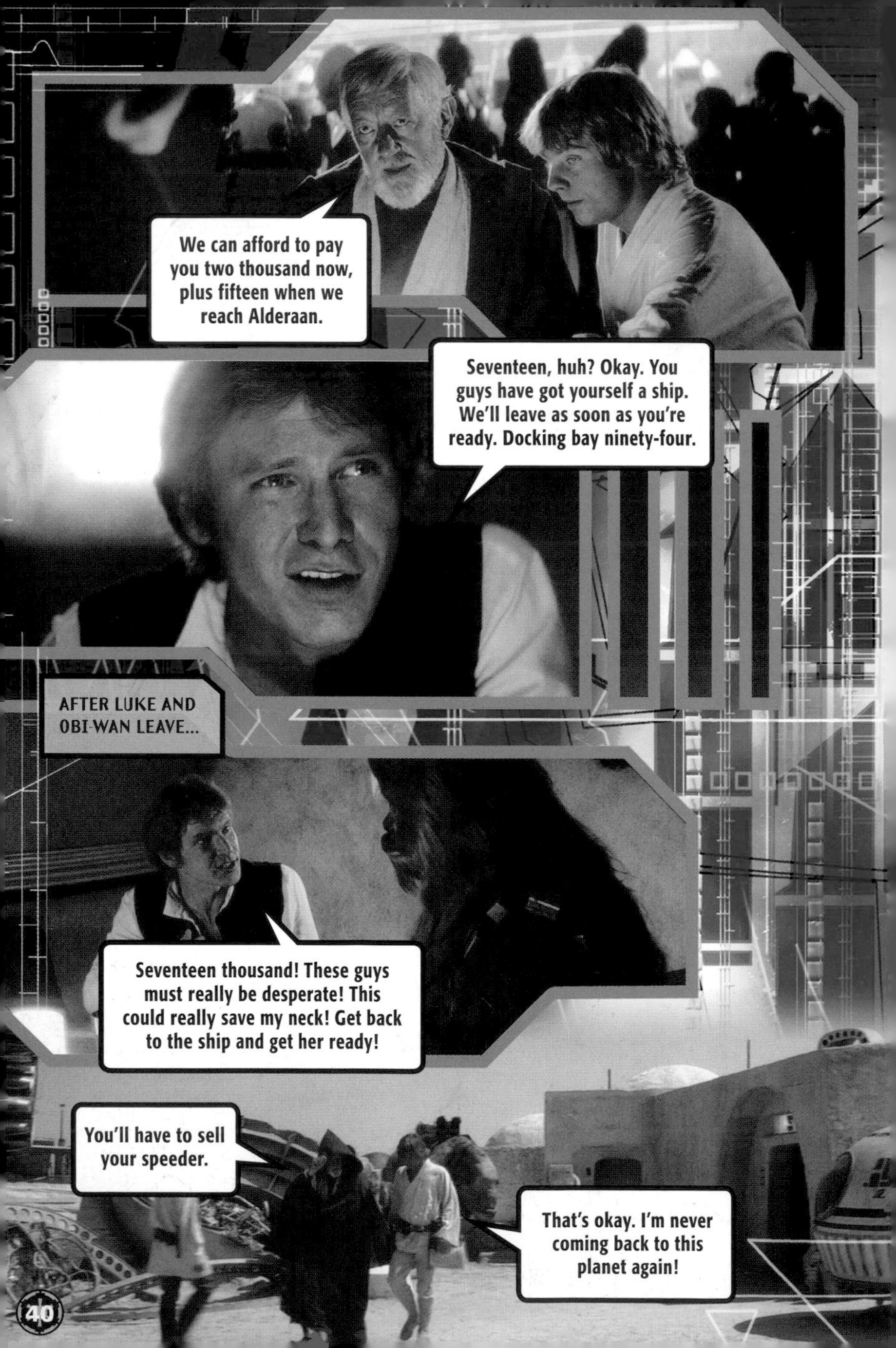

We can afford to pay you two thousand now, plus fifteen when we reach Alderaan.
Seventeen, huh? Okay. You guys have got yourself a ship. We'll leave as soon as you're ready. Docking bay ninety-four.
AFTER LUKE AND OBI-WAN LEAVE...
Seventeen thousand! These guys must really be desperate! This could really save my neck! Get back to the ship and get her ready!
You'll have to sell your speeder.
That's okay. I'm never coming back to this planet again!

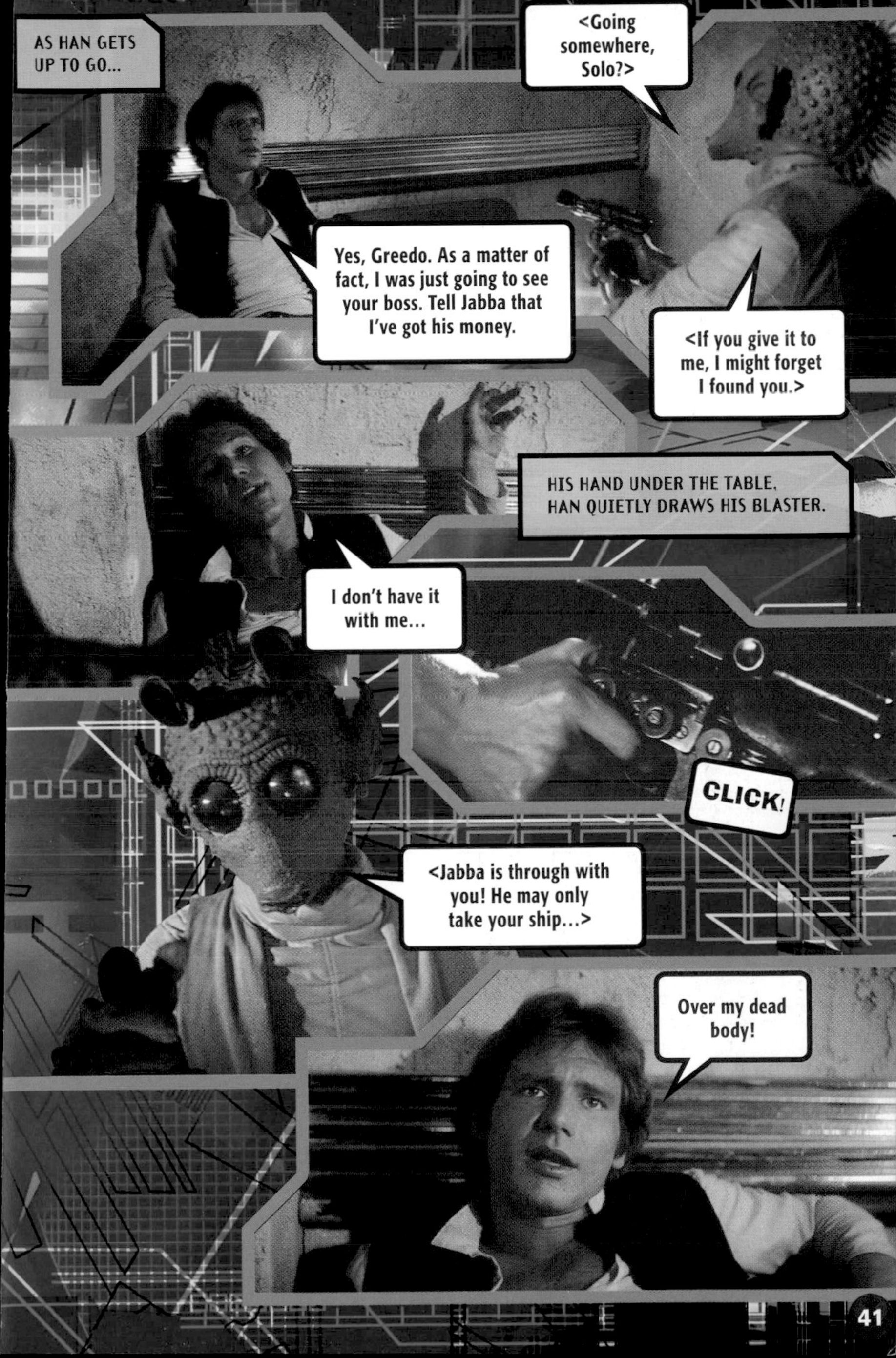
AS HAN GETS UP TO GO...
<Going somewhere, Solo?>
Yes, Greedo. As a matter of fact, I was just going to see your boss. Tell Jabba that I've got his money.
<If you give it to me, I might forget I found you.>
HIS HAND UNDER THE TABLE, HAN QUIETLY DRAWS HIS BLASTER.
I don't have it with me...
CLICK!
<Jabba is through with you! He may only take your ship...>
Over my dead body!

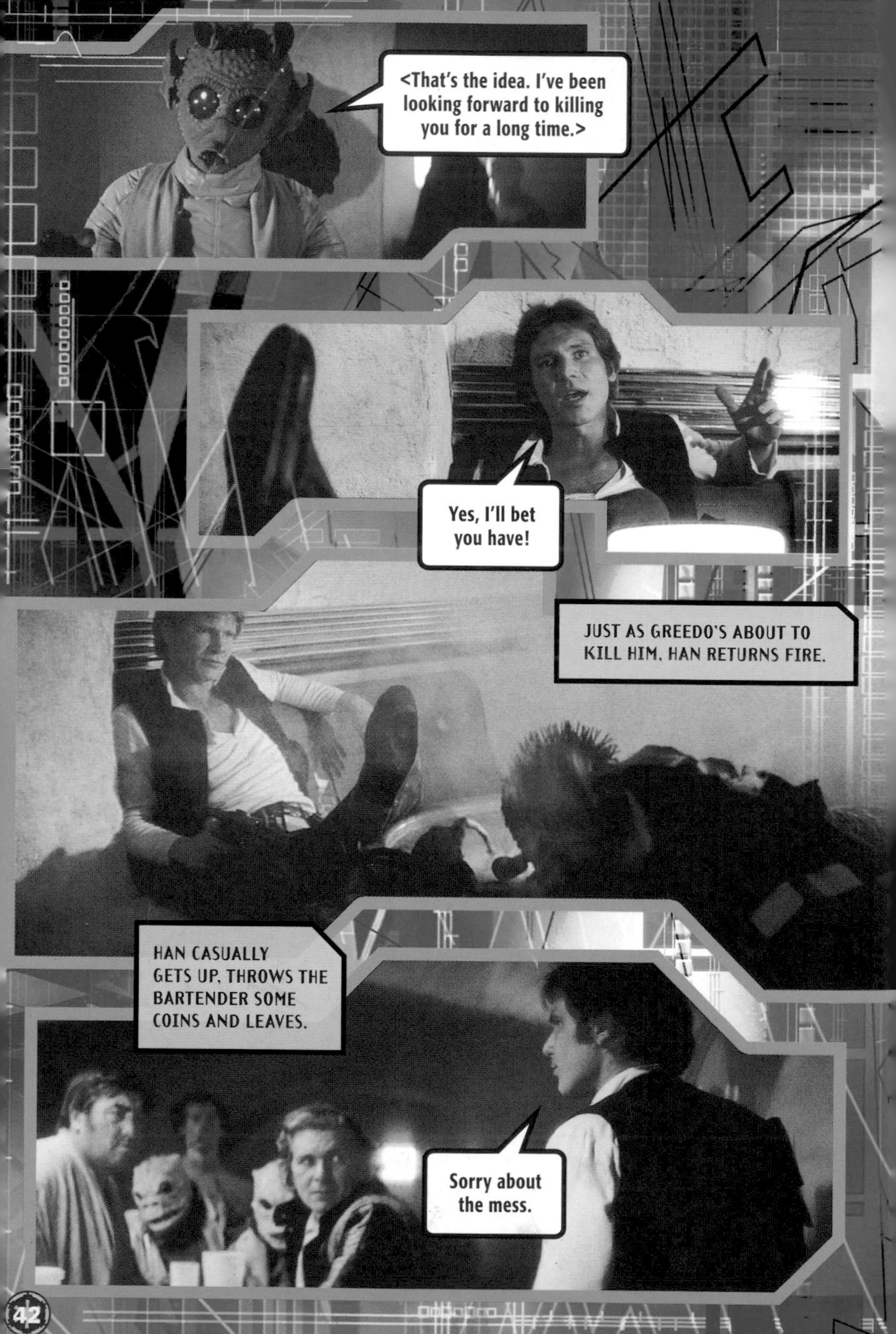
<That's the idea. I've been looking forward to killing you for a long time.>
Yes, I'll bet you have!
JUST AS GREEDO'S ABOUT TO KILL HIM, HAN RETURNS FIRE.
HAN CASUALLY GETS UP, THROWS THE BARTENDER SOME COINS AND LEAVES.
Sorry about the mess.

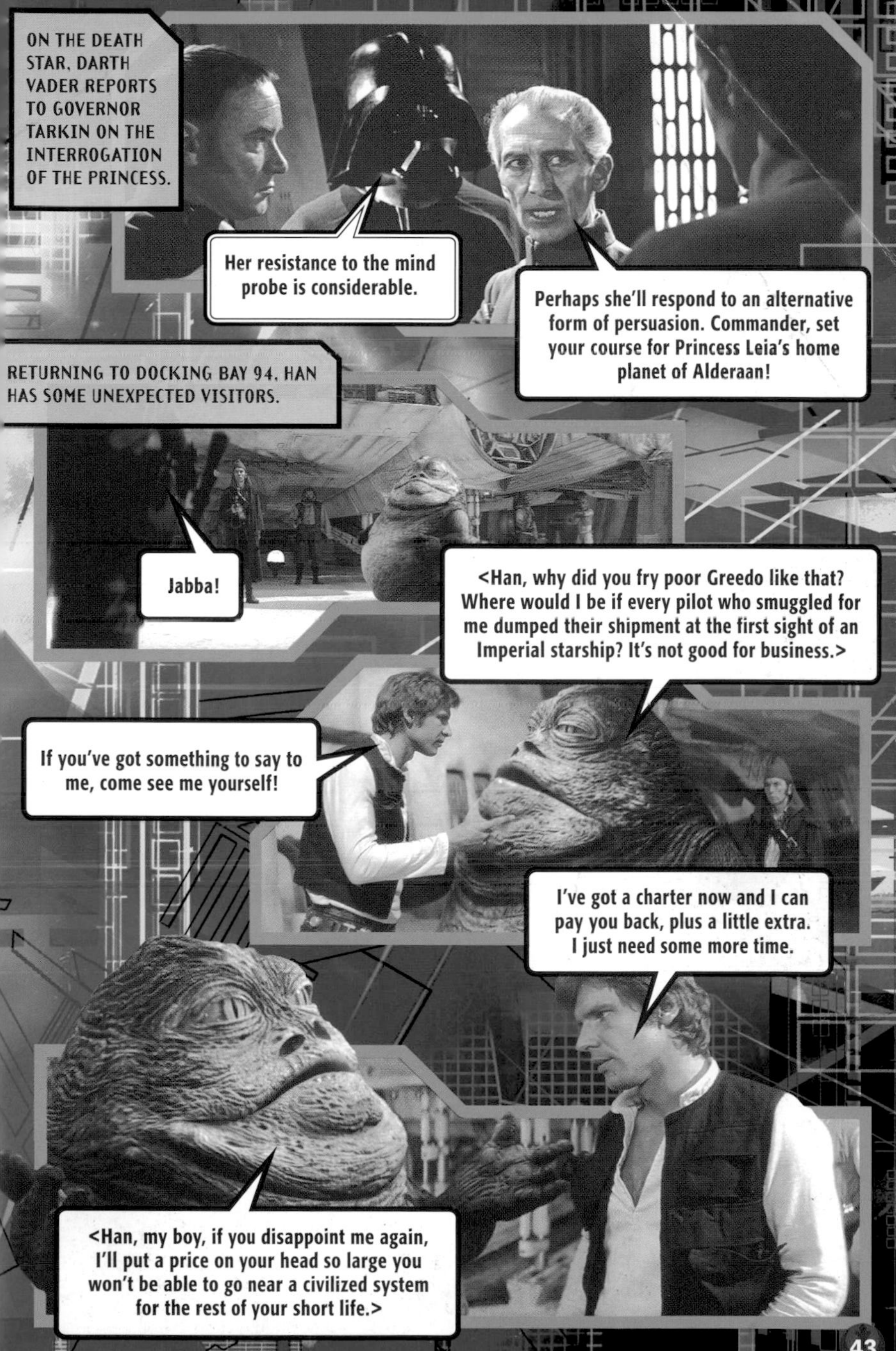
ON THE DEATH STAR, DARTH VADER REPORTS TO GOVERNOR TARKIN ON THE INTERROGATION OF THE PRINCESS.
Her resistance to the mind probe is considerable.
Perhaps she'll respond to an alternative form of persuasion. Commander, set your course for Princess Leia's home planet of Alderaan!
RETURNING TO DOCKING BAY 94, HAN HAS SOME UNEXPECTED VISITORS.
Jabba!
<Han, why did you fry poor Greedo like that? Where would I be if every pilot who smuggled for me dumped their shipment at the first sight of an Imperial starship? It's not good for business.>
If you've got something to say to me, come see me yourself!
I've got a charter now and I can pay you back, plus a little extra. I just need some more time.
<Han, my boy, if you disappoint me again, I'll put a price on your head so large you won't be able to go near a civilized system for the rest of your short life.>

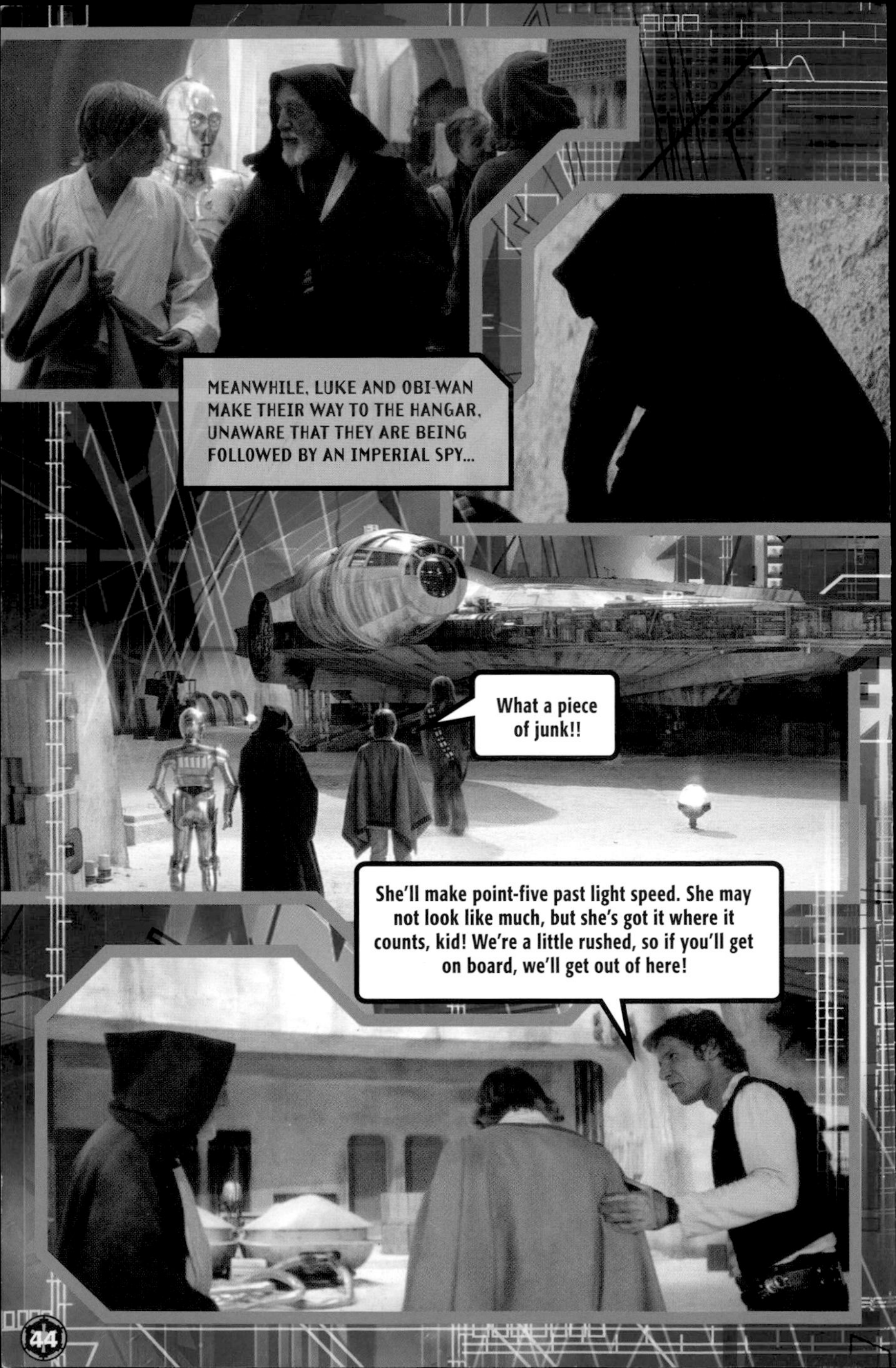
MEANWHILE, LUKE AND OBI-WAN MAKE THEIR WAY TO THE HANGAR, UNAWARE THAT THEY ARE BEING FOLLOWED BY AN IMPERIAL SPY...
What a piece of junk!!
She'll make point-five past light speed. She may not look like much, but she's got it where it counts, kid! We're a little rushed, so if you'll get on board, we'll get out of here!

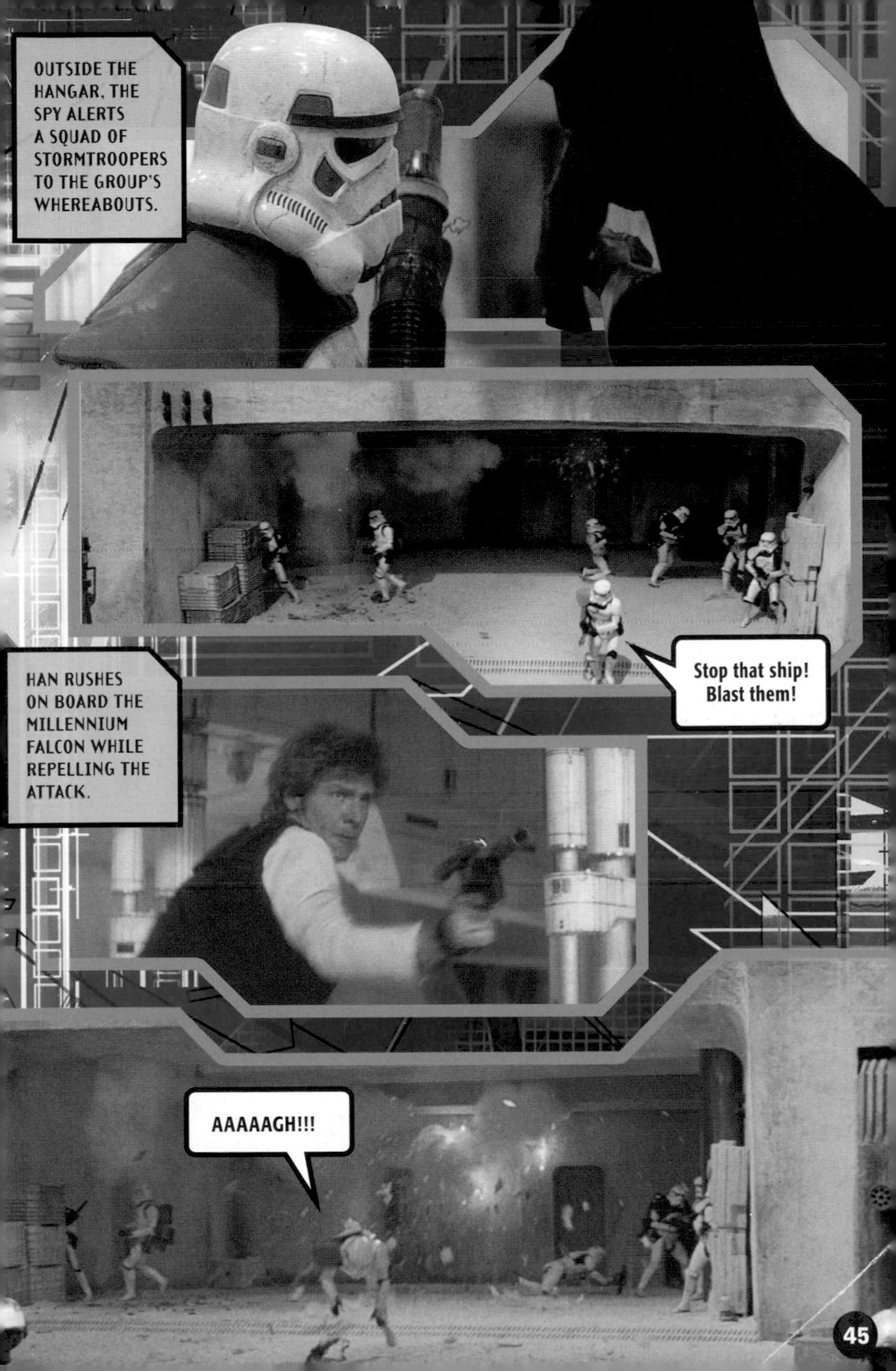
OUTSIDE THE HANGAR, THE SPY ALERTS A SQUAD OF STORMTROOPERS TO THE GROUP'S WHEREABOUTS.
Stop that ship! Blast them!
HAN RUSHES ON BOARD THE MILLENNIUM FALCON WHILE REPELLING THE ATTACK.
AAAAAGH!!!

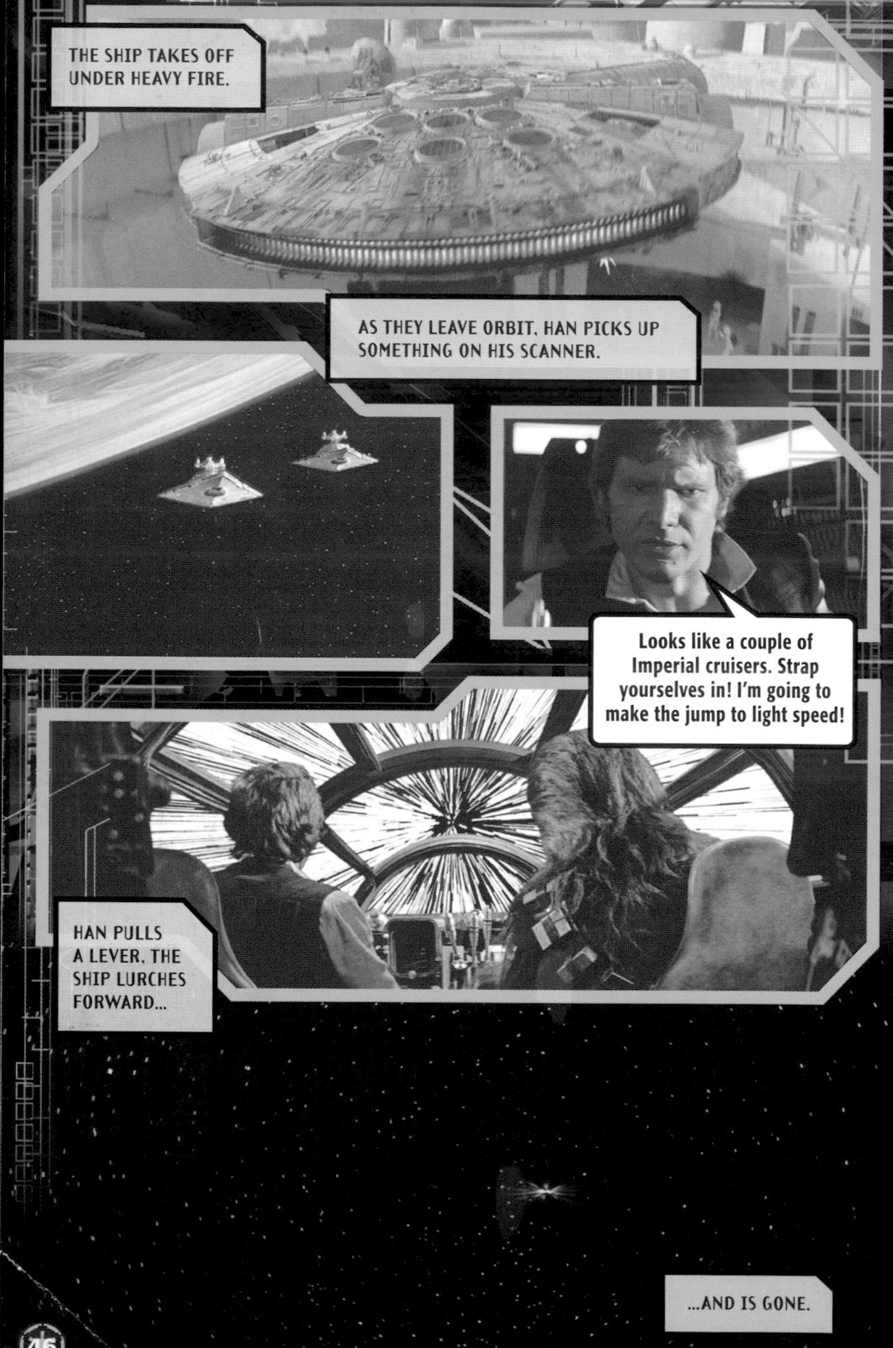
THE SHIP TAKES OFF UNDER HEAVY FIRE.
AS THEY LEAVE ORBIT, HAN PICKS UP SOMETHING ON HIS SCANNER.
Looks like a couple of Imperial cruisers. Strap yourselves in! I'm going to make the jump to light speed!
HAN PULLS A LEVER, THE SHIP LURCHES FORWARD...
...AND IS GONE.

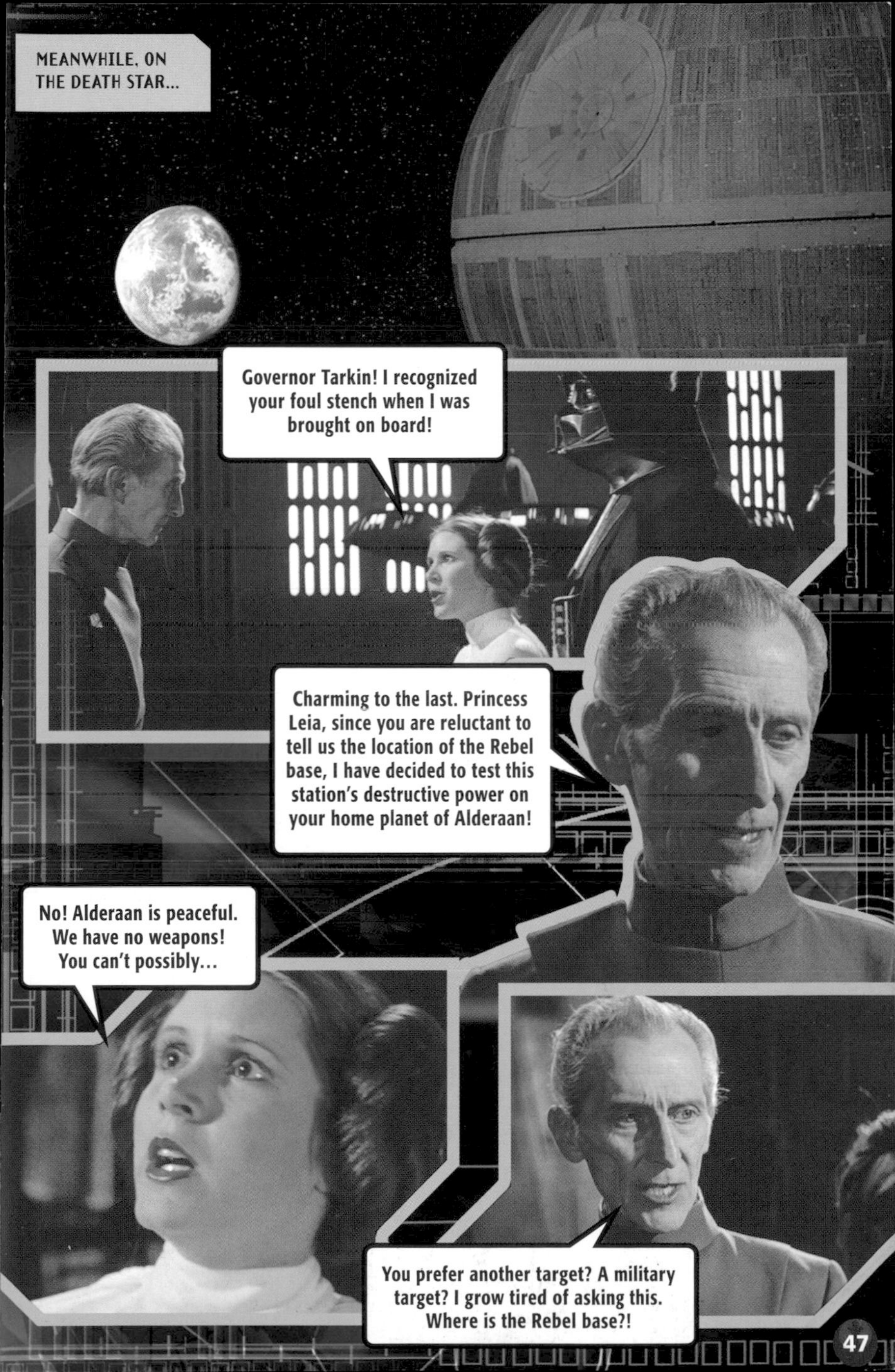
MEANWHILE, ON THE DEATH STAR...
Governor Tarkin! I recognized your foul stench when I was brought on board!
Charming to the last. Princess Leia, since you are reluctant to tell us the location of the Rebel base, I have decided to test this station's destructive power on your home planet of Alderaan!
No! Alderaan is peaceful. We have no weapons! You can't possibly...
You prefer another target? A military target? I grow tired of asking this. Where is the Rebel base?!

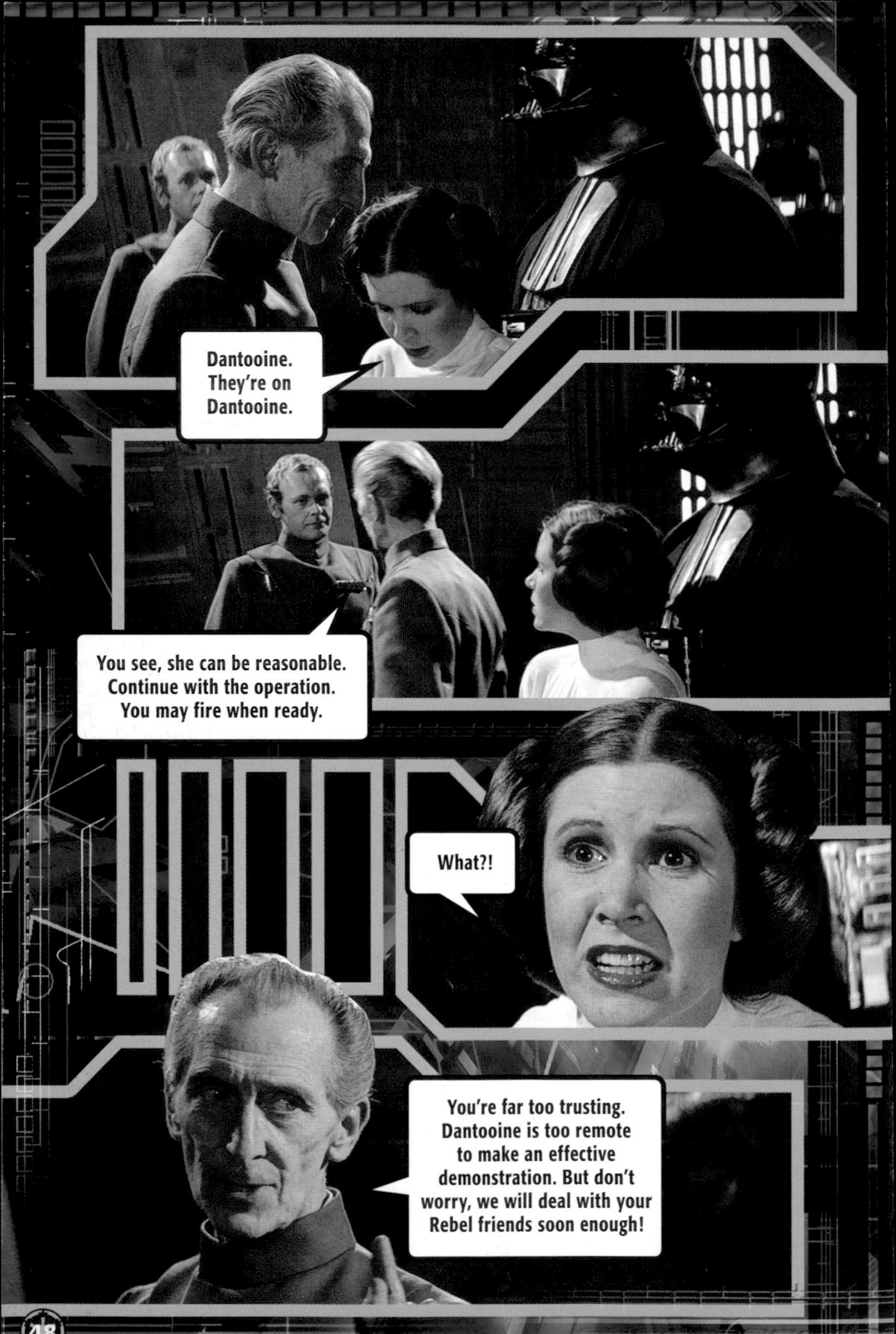

Dantooine. They're on Dantooine.
You see, she can be reasonable. Continue with the operation. You may fire when ready.
What?!
You're far too trusting. Dantooine is too remote to make an effective demonstration. But don't worry, we will deal with your Rebel friends soon enough!

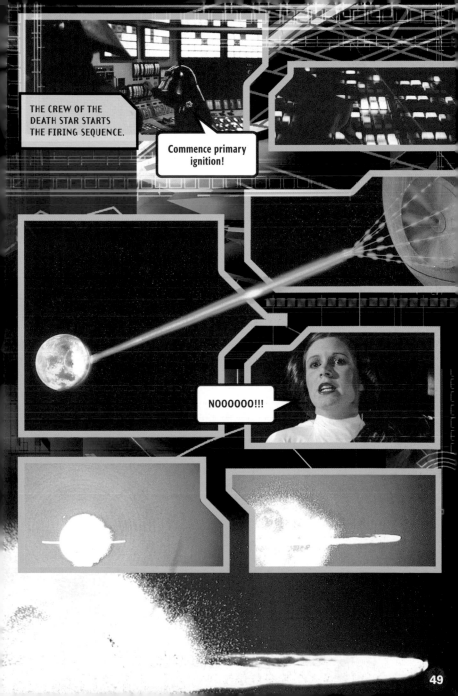

THE CREW OF THE DEATH STAR STARTS THE FIRING SEQUENCE.

Commence primary ignition!

NOOOOOO!!!

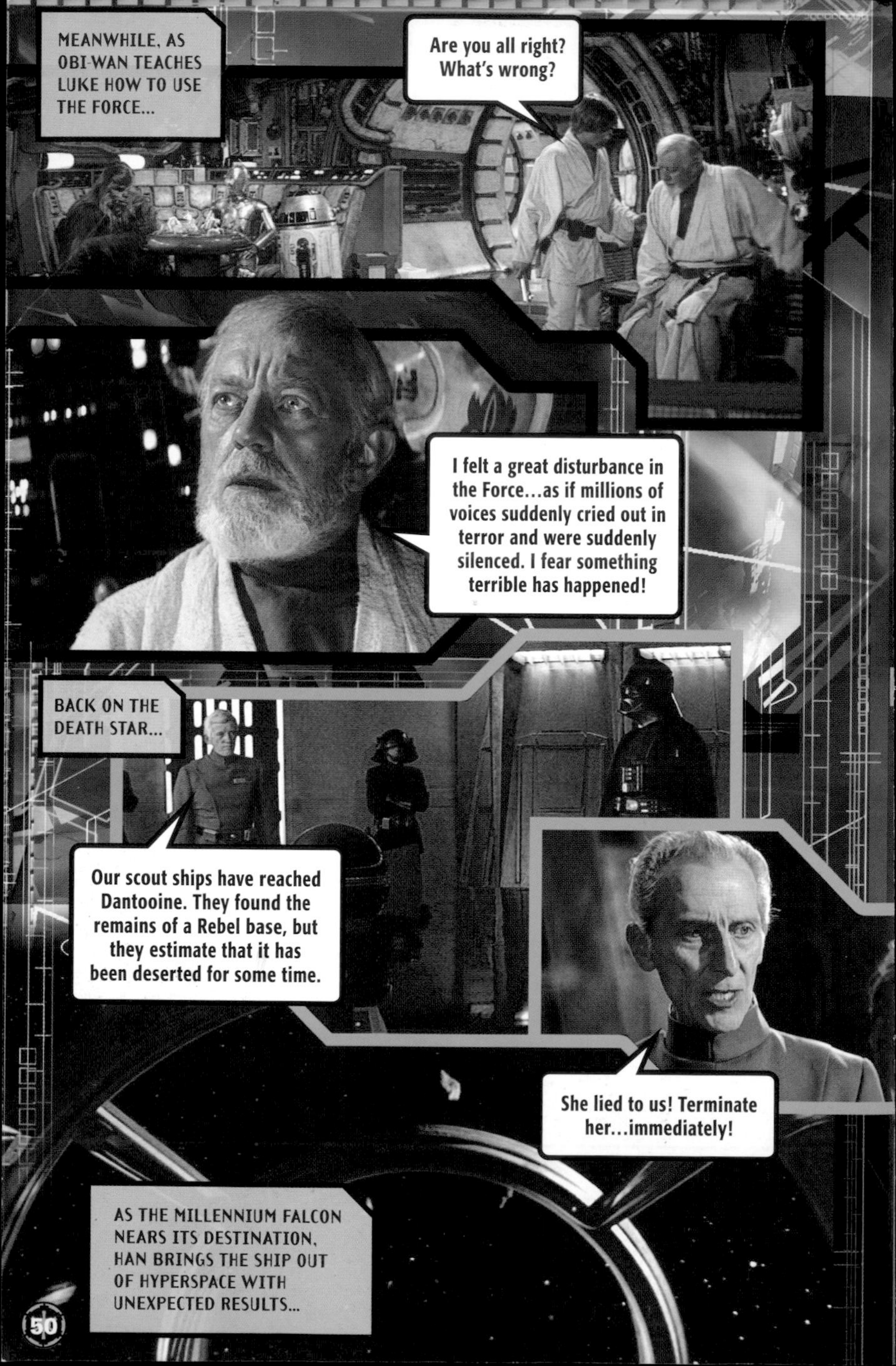
MEANWHILE, AS OBI-WAN TEACHES LUKE HOW TO USE THE FORCE...
Are you all right? What's wrong?
I felt a great disturbance in the Force...as if millions of voices suddenly cried out in terror and were suddenly silenced. I fear something terrible has happened!
BACK ON THE DEATH STAR...
Our scout ships have reached Dantooine. They found the remains of a Rebel base, but they estimate that it has been deserted for some time.
She lied to us! Terminate her...immediately!
AS THE MILLENNIUM FALCON NEARS ITS DESTINATION, HAN BRINGS THE SHIP OUT OF HYPERSPACE WITH UNEXPECTED RESULTS...

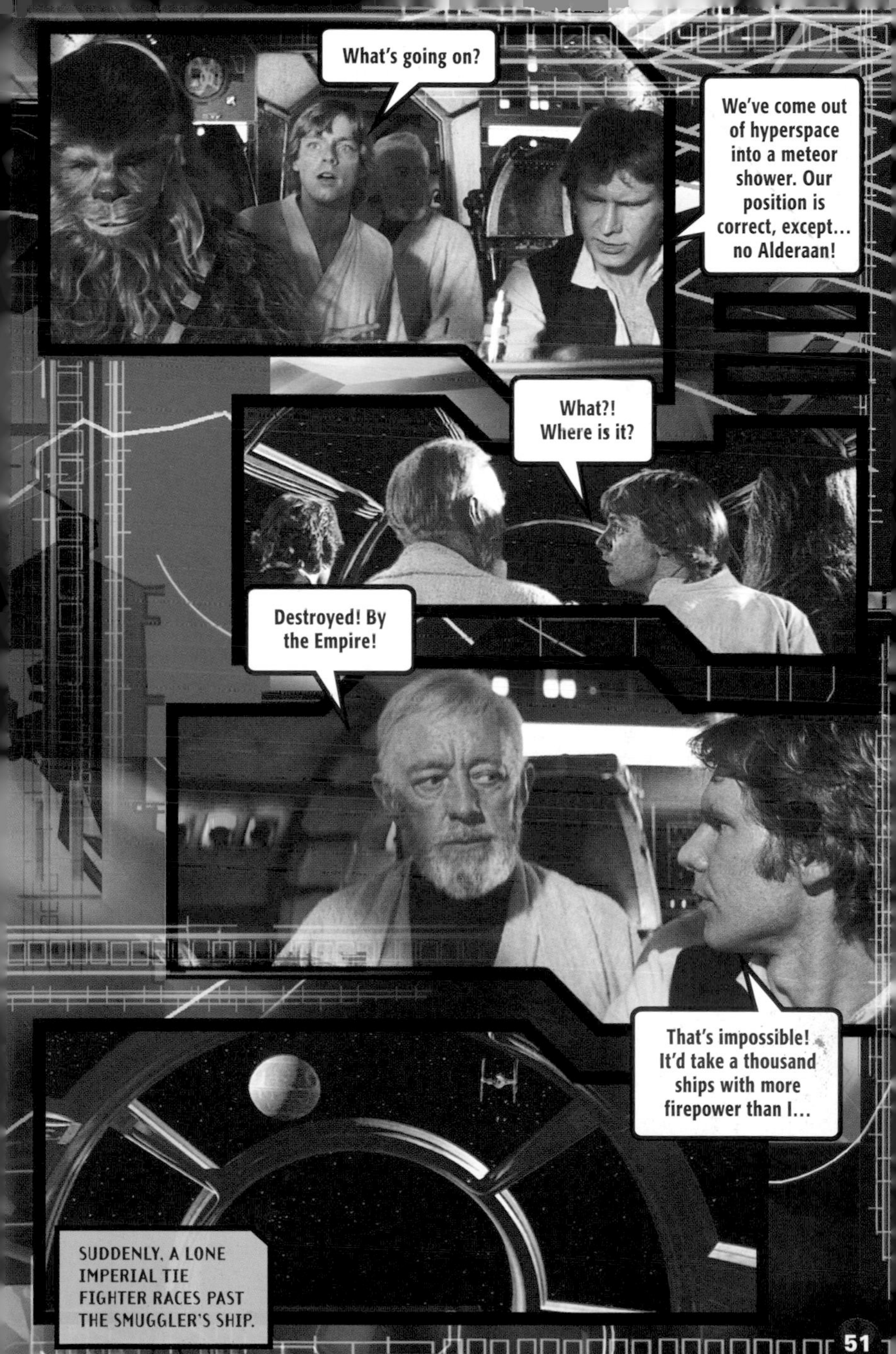

What's going on?
We've come out of hyperspace into a meteor shower. Our position is correct, except... no Alderaan!
What?! Where is it?
Destroyed! By the Empire!
That's impossible! It'd take a thousand ships with more firepower than I...
SUDDENLY, A LONE IMPERIAL TIE FIGHTER RACES PAST THE SMUGGLER'S SHIP.

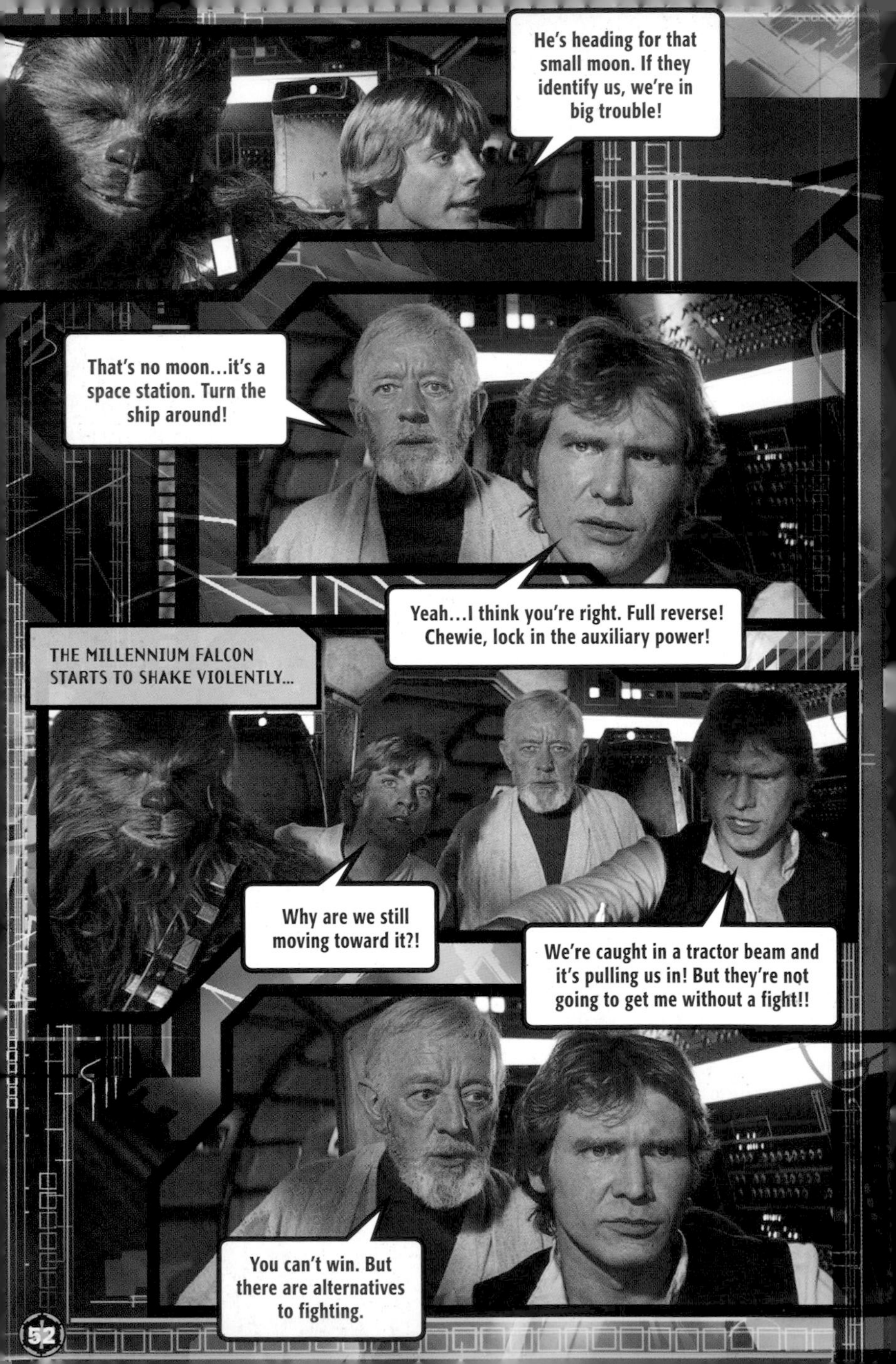

He's heading for that small moon. If they identify us, we're in big trouble!
That's no moon…it's a space station. Turn the ship around!
Yeah…I think you're right. Full reverse! Chewie, lock in the auxiliary power!
THE MILLENNIUM FALCON STARTS TO SHAKE VIOLENTLY…
Why are we still moving toward it?!
We're caught in a tractor beam and it's pulling us in! But they're not going to get me without a fight!!
You can't win. But there are alternatives to fighting.

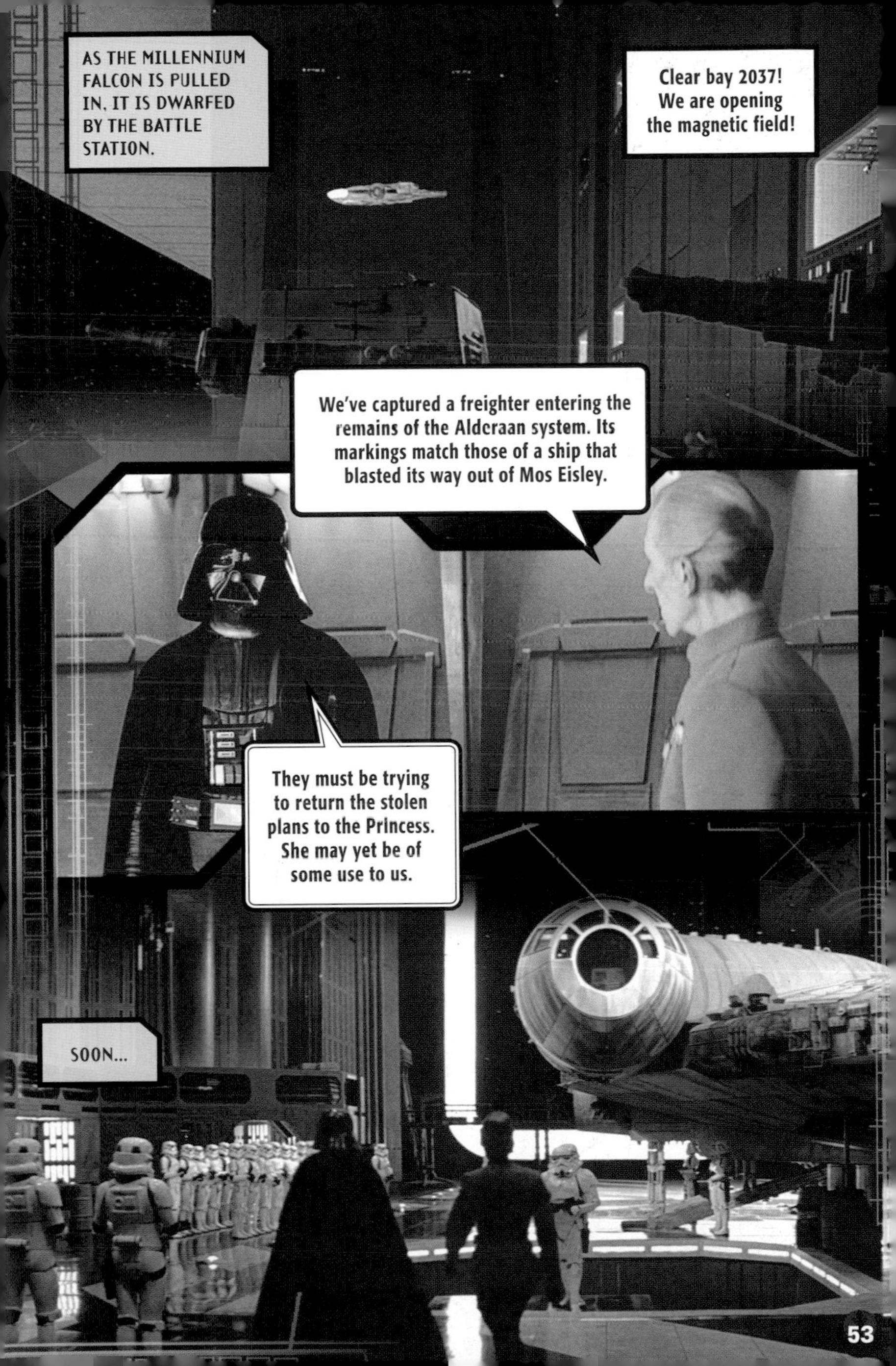
AS THE MILLENNIUM FALCON IS PULLED IN, IT IS DWARFED BY THE BATTLE STATION.
Clear bay 2037! We are opening the magnetic field!
We've captured a freighter entering the remains of the Alderaan system. Its markings match those of a ship that blasted its way out of Mos Eisley.
They must be trying to return the stolen plans to the Princess. She may yet be of some use to us.
SOON...

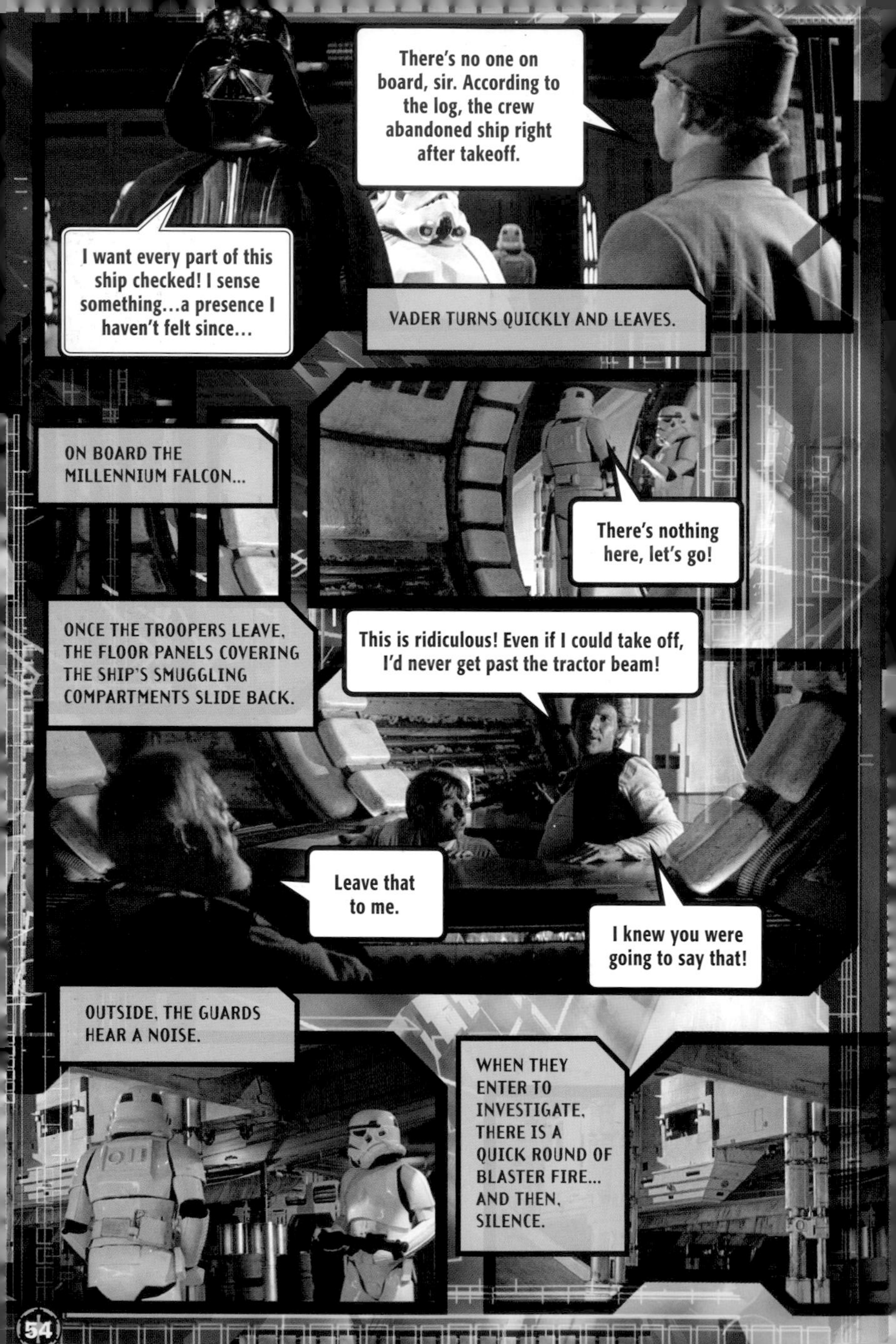
There's no one on board, sir. According to the log, the crew abandoned ship right after takeoff.
I want every part of this ship checked! I sense something...a presence I haven't felt since...
VADER TURNS QUICKLY AND LEAVES.
ON BOARD THE MILLENNIUM FALCON...
There's nothing here, let's go!
ONCE THE TROOPERS LEAVE, THE FLOOR PANELS COVERING THE SHIP'S SMUGGLING COMPARTMENTS SLIDE BACK.
This is ridiculous! Even if I could take off, I'd never get past the tractor beam!
Leave that to me.
I knew you were going to say that!
OUTSIDE, THE GUARDS HEAR A NOISE.
WHEN THEY ENTER TO INVESTIGATE, THERE IS A QUICK ROUND OF BLASTER FIRE... AND THEN, SILENCE.

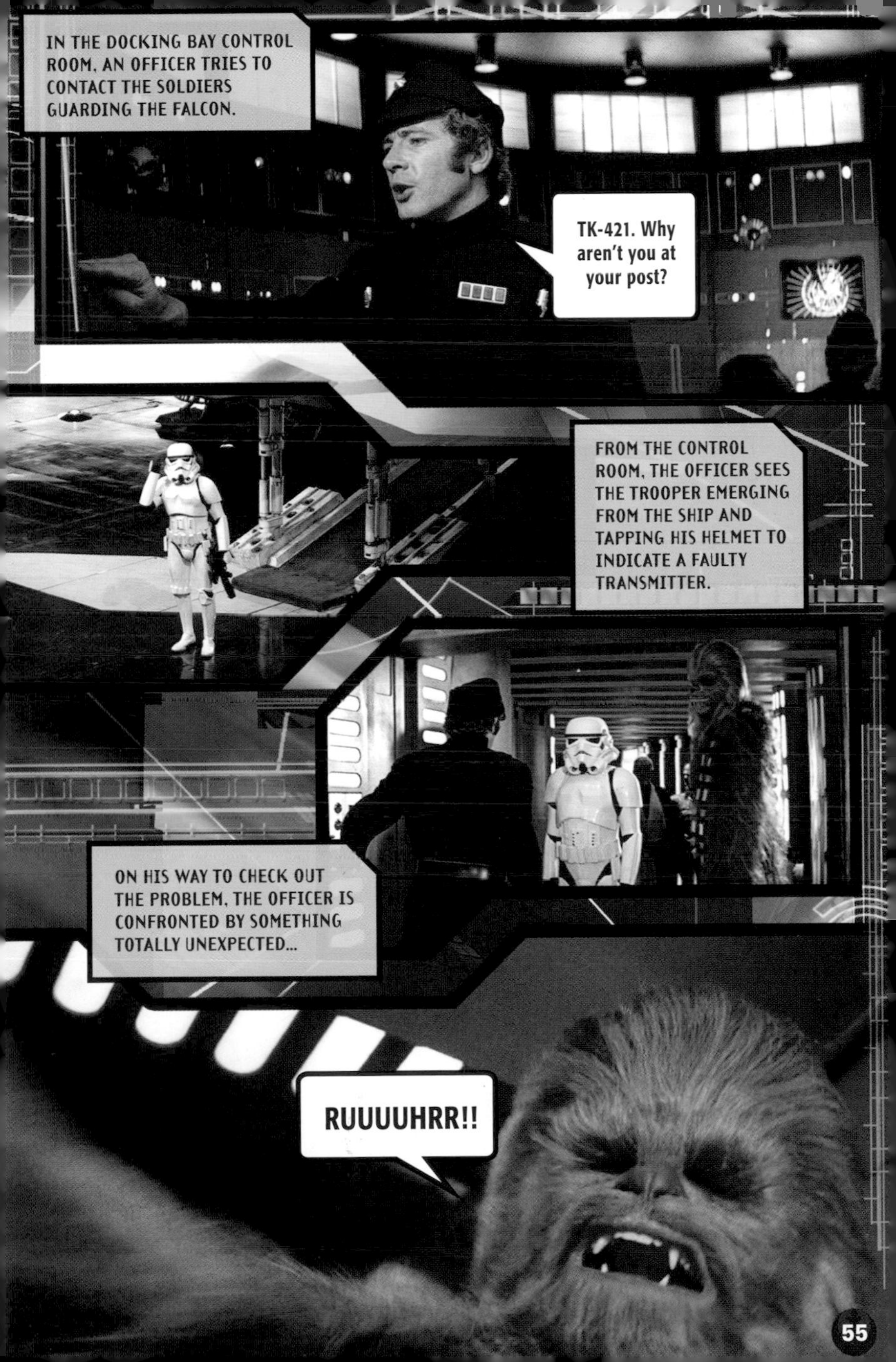
IN THE DOCKING BAY CONTROL ROOM, AN OFFICER TRIES TO CONTACT THE SOLDIERS GUARDING THE FALCON.
TK-421. Why aren't you at your post?
FROM THE CONTROL ROOM, THE OFFICER SEES THE TROOPER EMERGING FROM THE SHIP AND TAPPING HIS HELMET TO INDICATE A FAULTY TRANSMITTER.
ON HIS WAY TO CHECK OUT THE PROBLEM, THE OFFICER IS CONFRONTED BY SOMETHING TOTALLY UNEXPECTED...
RUUUUHRR!!

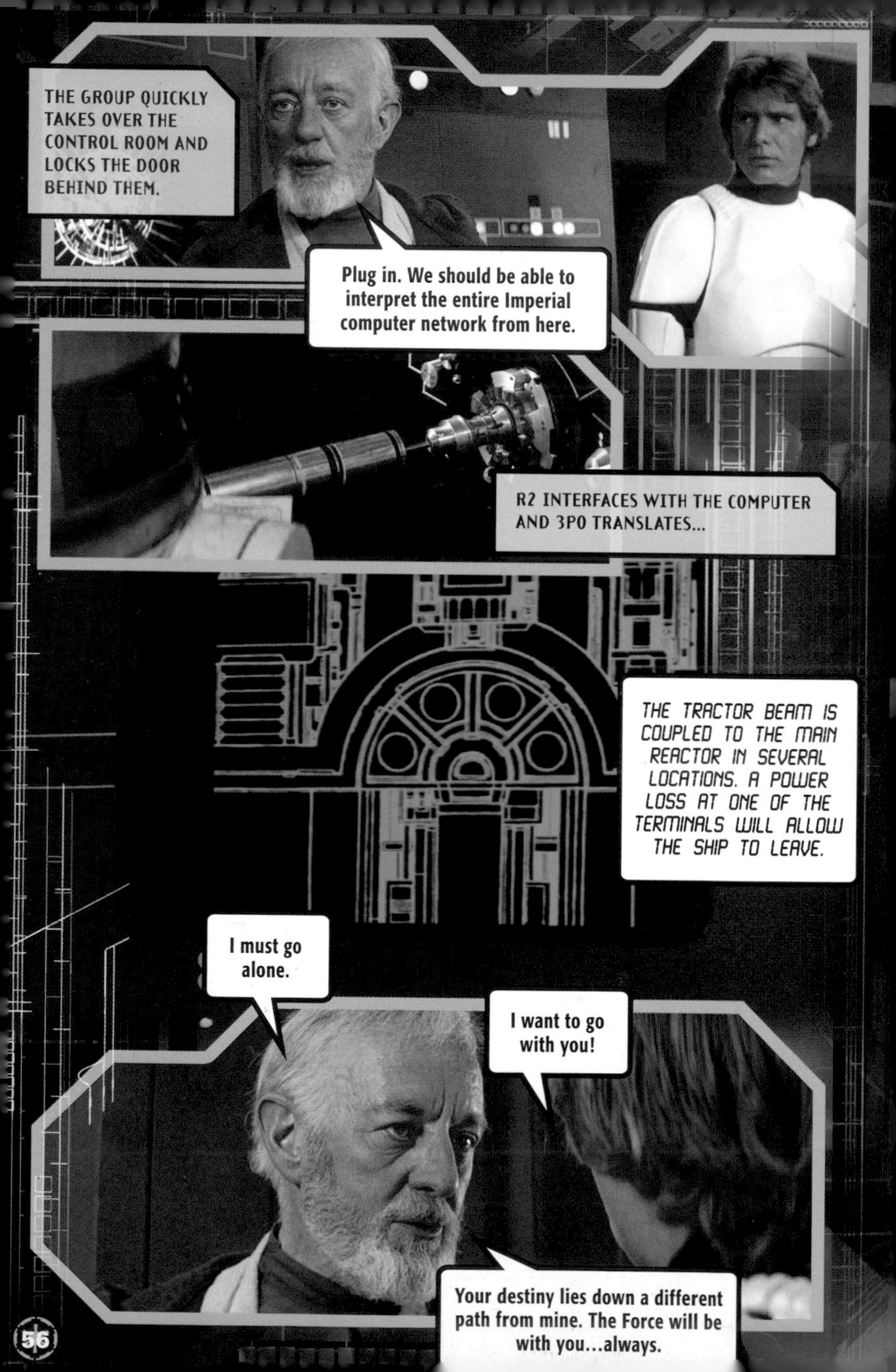
THE GROUP QUICKLY TAKES OVER THE CONTROL ROOM AND LOCKS THE DOOR BEHIND THEM.
Plug in. We should be able to interpret the entire Imperial computer network from here.
R2 INTERFACES WITH THE COMPUTER AND 3PO TRANSLATES...
THE TRACTOR BEAM IS COUPLED TO THE MAIN REACTOR IN SEVERAL LOCATIONS. A POWER LOSS AT ONE OF THE TERMINALS WILL ALLOW THE SHIP TO LEAVE.
I must go alone.
I want to go with you!
Your destiny lies down a different path from mine. The Force will be with you...always.

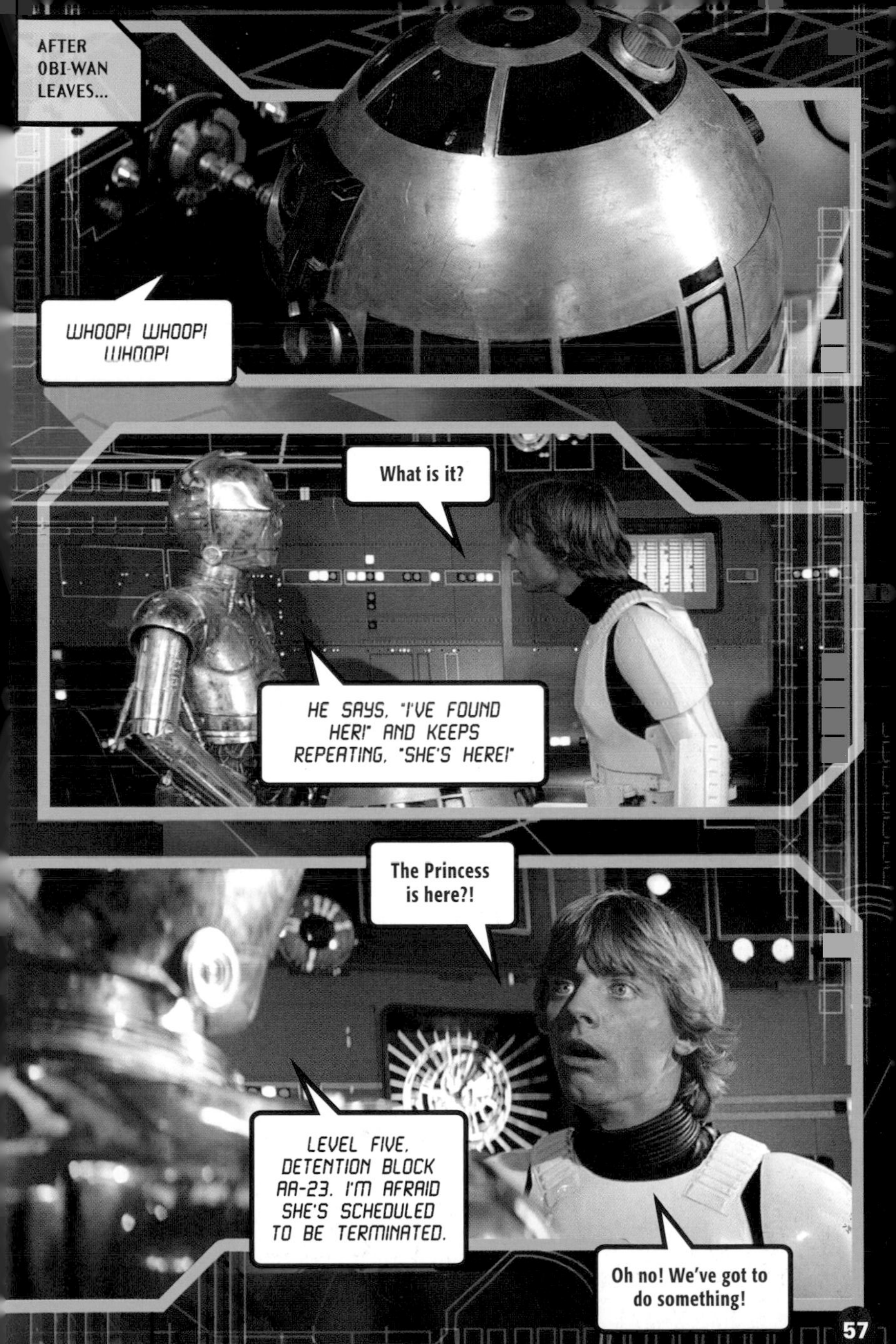
AFTER OBI-WAN LEAVES...
WHOOP! WHOOP! WHOOP!
What is it?
HE SAYS, "I'VE FOUND HER!" AND KEEPS REPEATING, "SHE'S HERE!"
The Princess is here?!
LEVEL FIVE, DETENTION BLOCK AA-23. I'M AFRAID SHE'S SCHEDULED TO BE TERMINATED.
Oh no! We've got to do something!

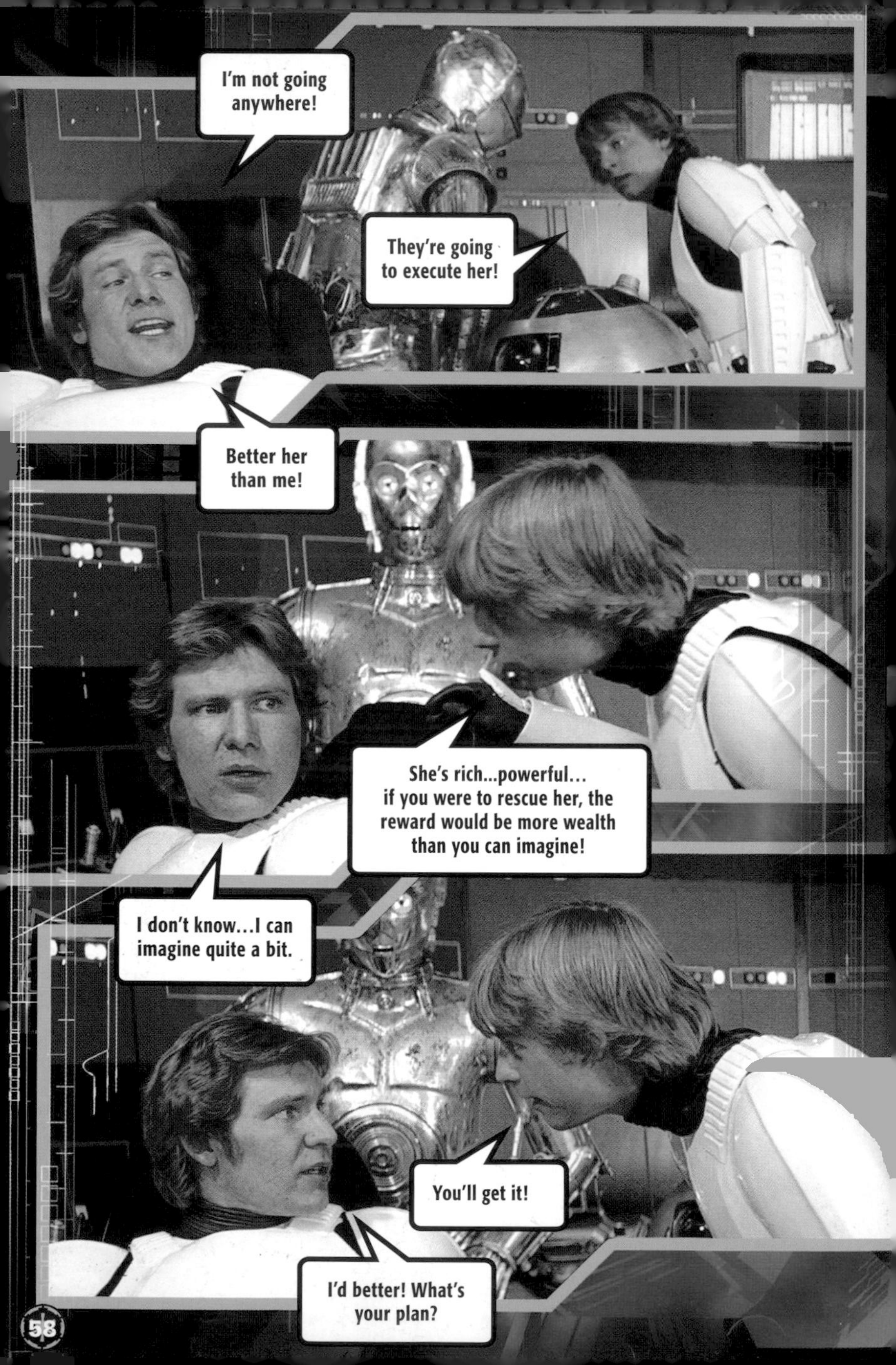
I'm not going anywhere!
They're going to execute her!
Better her than me!
She's rich...powerful... if you were to rescue her, the reward would be more wealth than you can imagine!
I don't know...I can imagine quite a bit.
You'll get it!
I'd better! What's your plan?

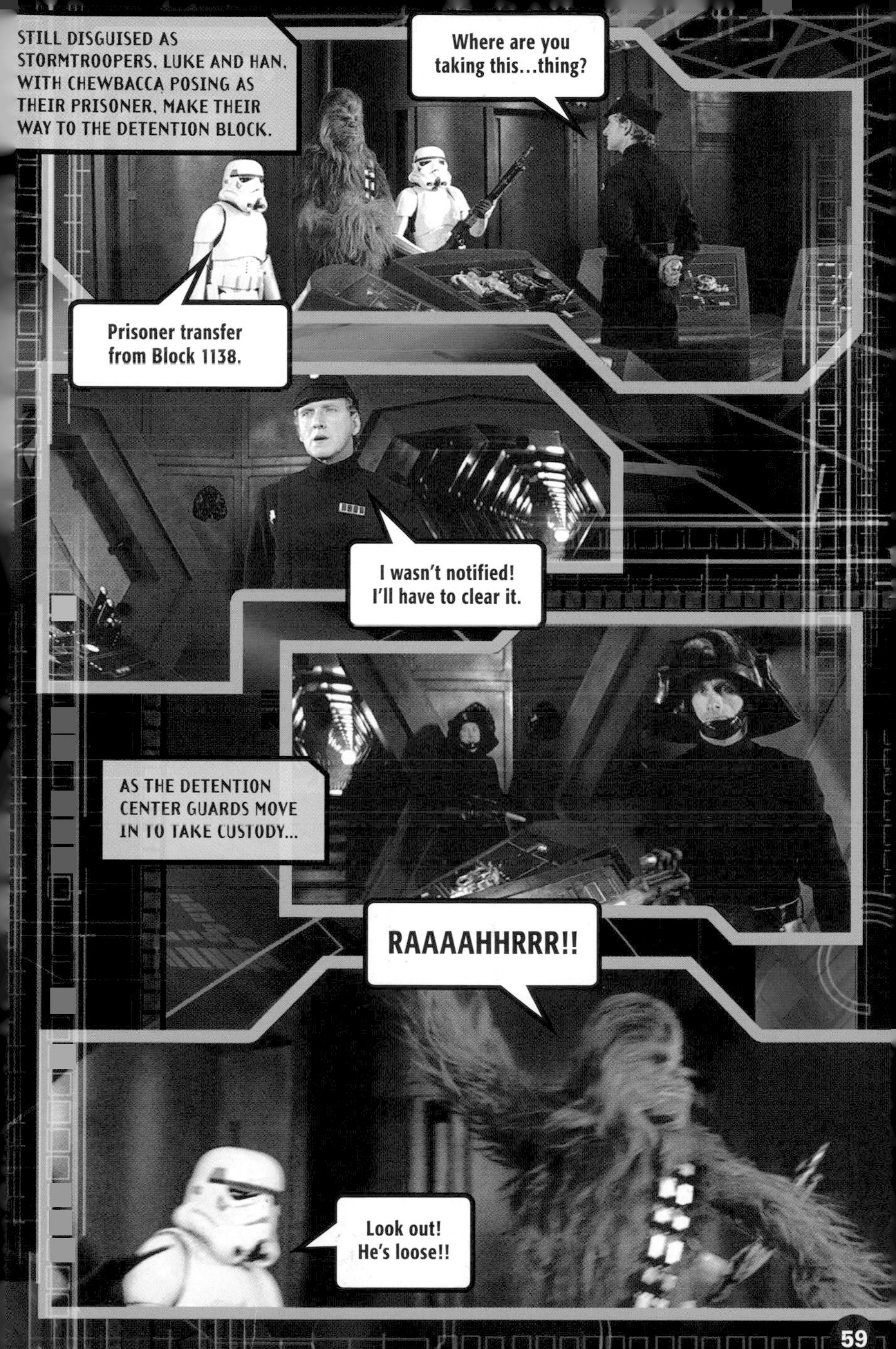
STILL DISGUISED AS STORMTROOPERS, LUKE AND HAN, WITH CHEWBACCA POSING AS THEIR PRISONER, MAKE THEIR WAY TO THE DETENTION BLOCK.
Where are you taking this...thing?
Prisoner transfer from Block 1138.
I wasn't notified! I'll have to clear it.
AS THE DETENTION CENTER GUARDS MOVE IN TO TAKE CUSTODY...
RAAAAHHRRR!!
Look out! He's loose!!

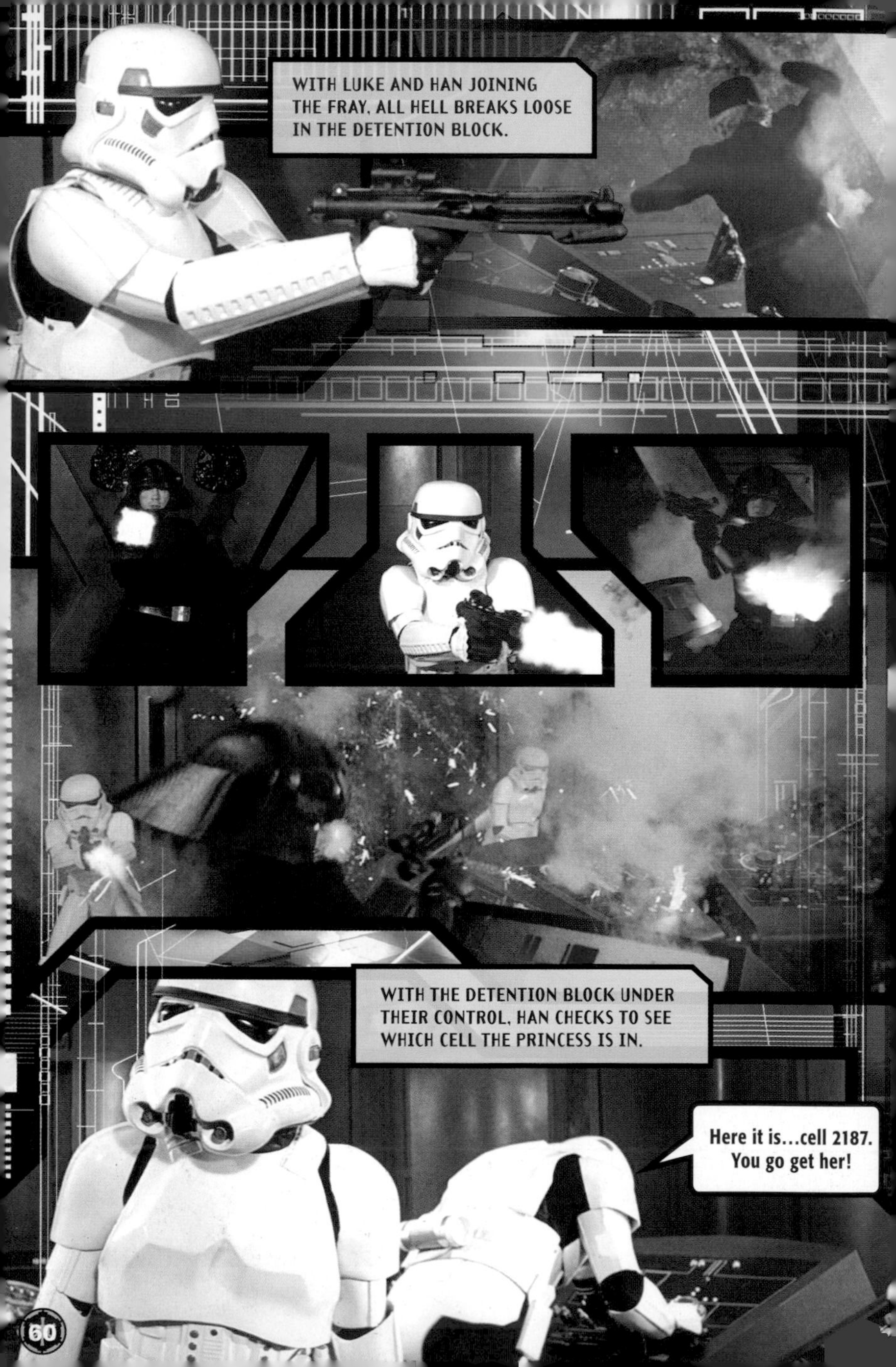
WITH LUKE AND HAN JOINING THE FRAY, ALL HELL BREAKS LOOSE IN THE DETENTION BLOCK.
WITH THE DETENTION BLOCK UNDER THEIR CONTROL, HAN CHECKS TO SEE WHICH CELL THE PRINCESS IS IN.
Here it is...cell 2187. You go get her!

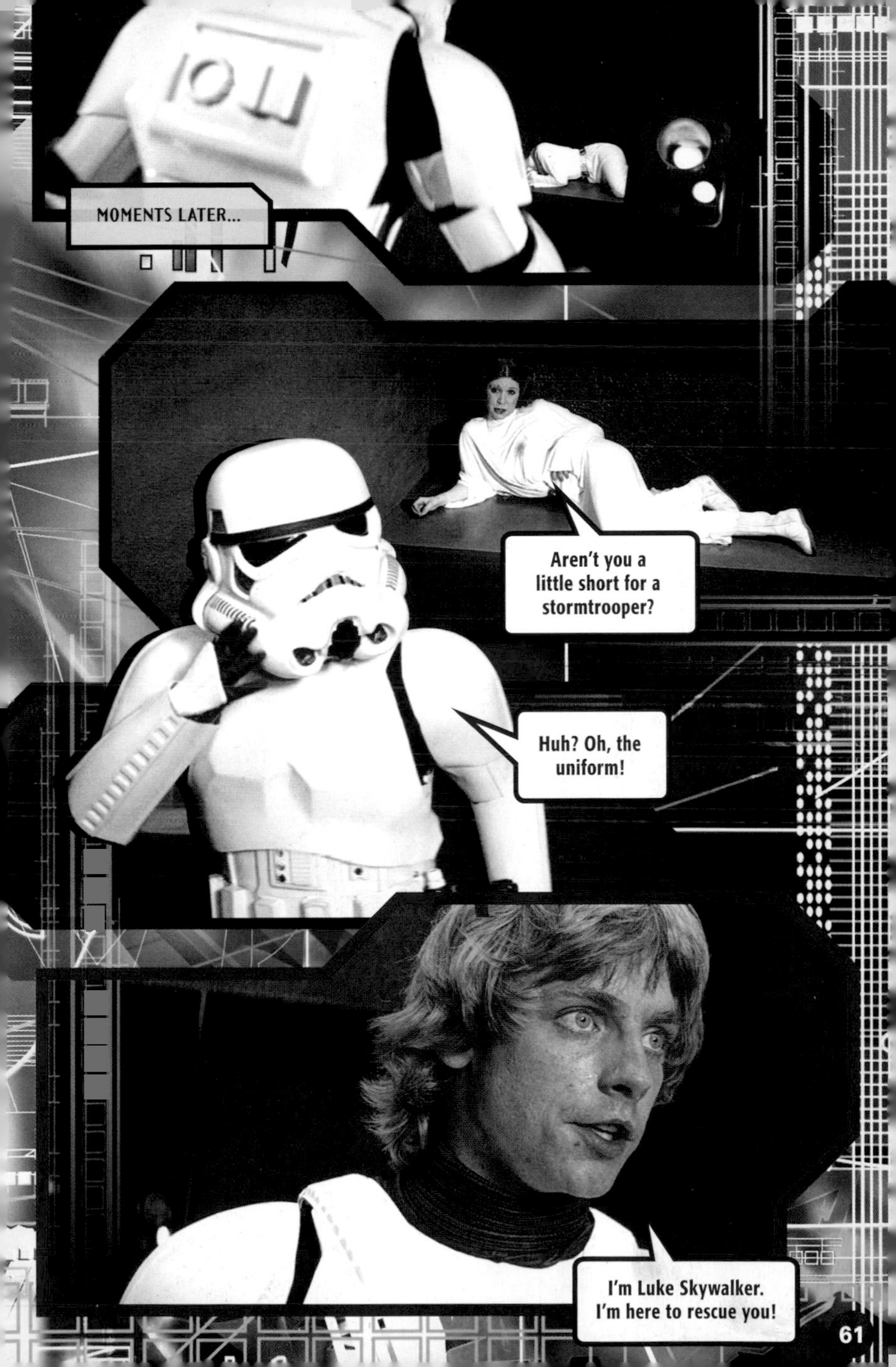
MOMENTS LATER...
Aren't you a little short for a stormtrooper?
Huh? Oh, the uniform!
I'm Luke Skywalker. I'm here to rescue you!

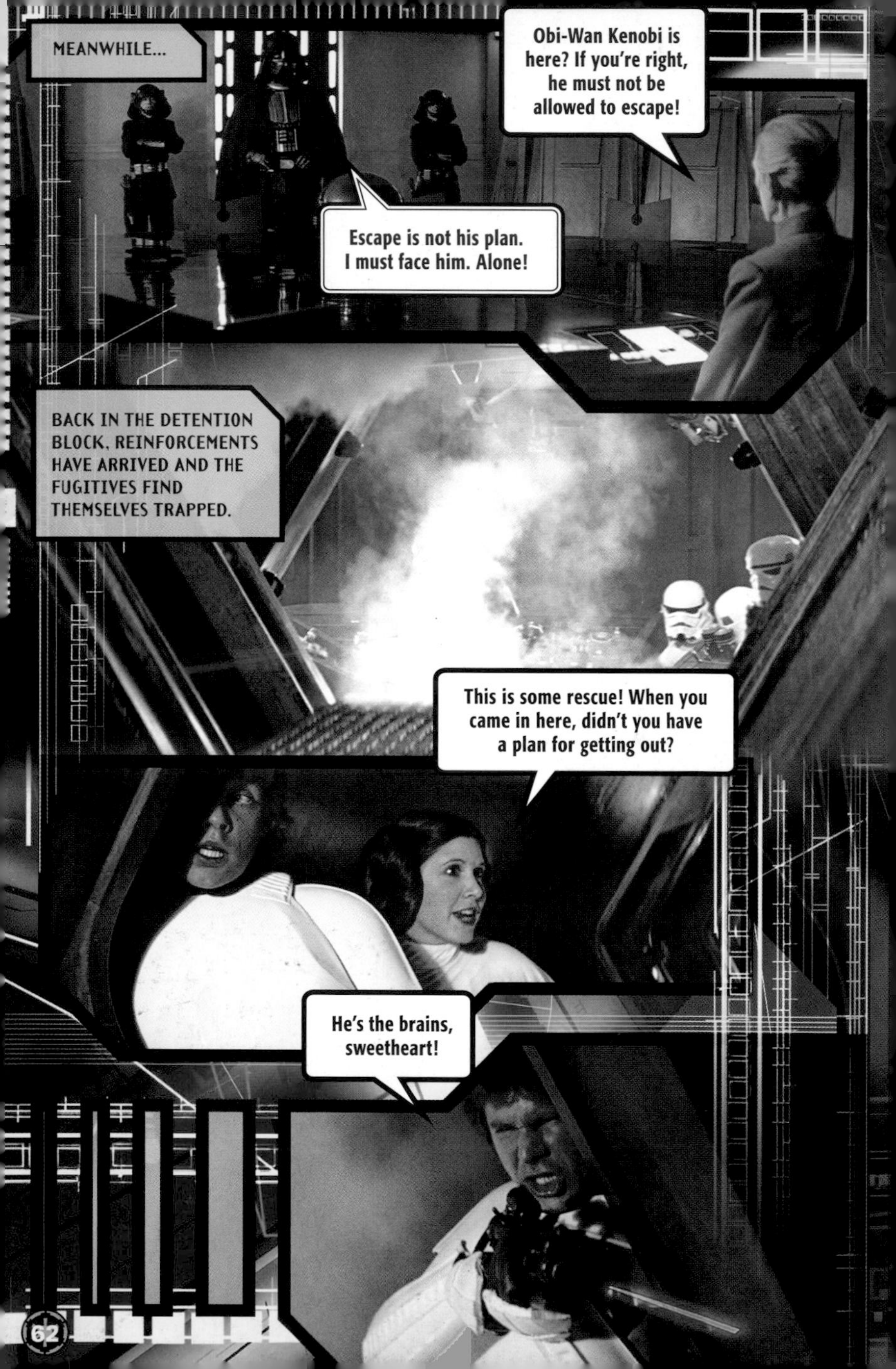
MEANWHILE...
Obi-Wan Kenobi is here? If you're right, he must not be allowed to escape!
Escape is not his plan. I must face him. Alone!
BACK IN THE DETENTION BLOCK, REINFORCEMENTS HAVE ARRIVED AND THE FUGITIVES FIND THEMSELVES TRAPPED.
This is some rescue! When you came in here, didn't you have a plan for getting out?
He's the brains, sweetheart!

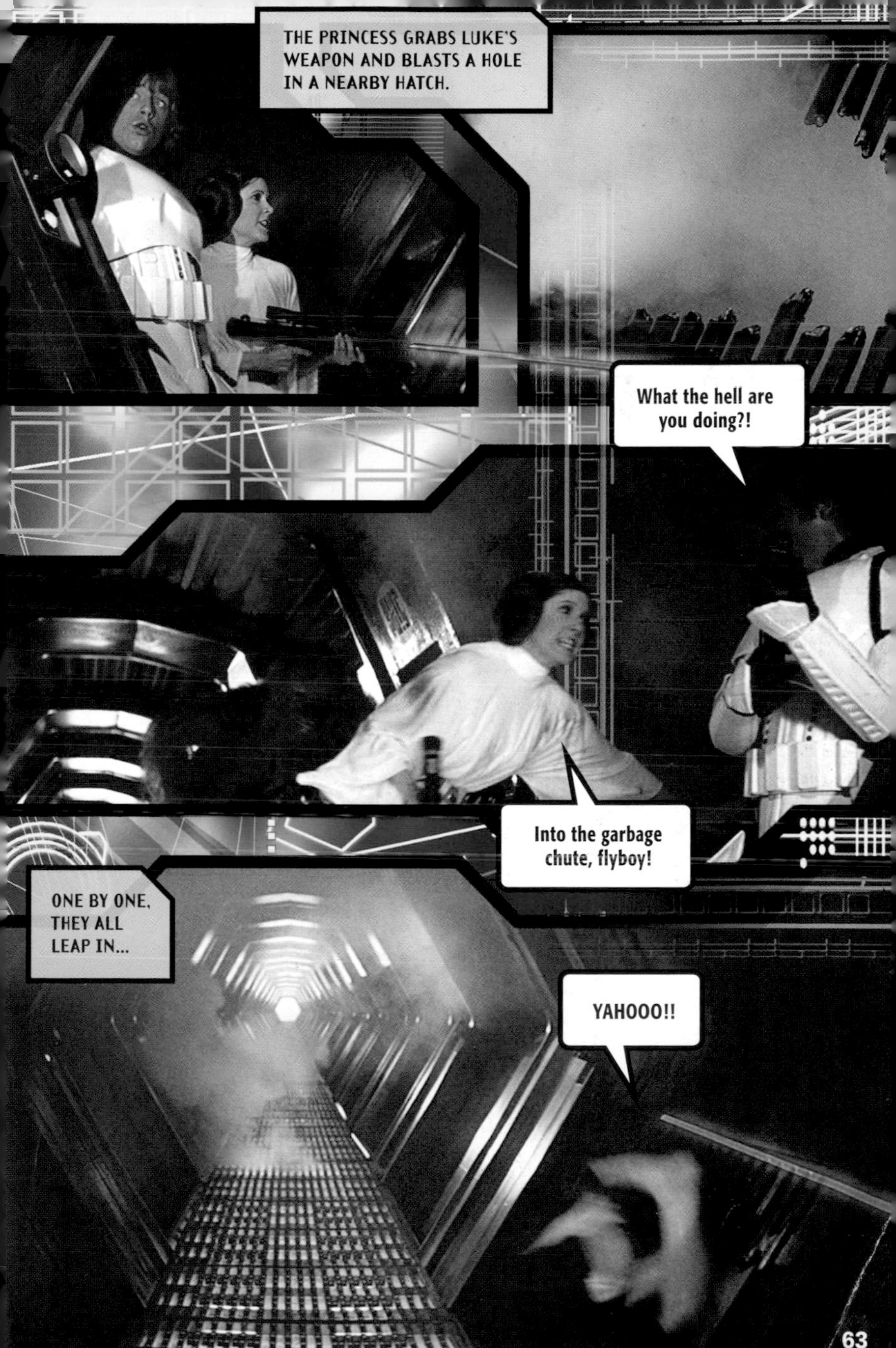
THE PRINCESS GRABS LUKE'S WEAPON AND BLASTS A HOLE IN A NEARBY HATCH.
What the hell are you doing?!
Into the garbage chute, flyboy!
ONE BY ONE, THEY ALL LEAP IN...
YAHOOO!!

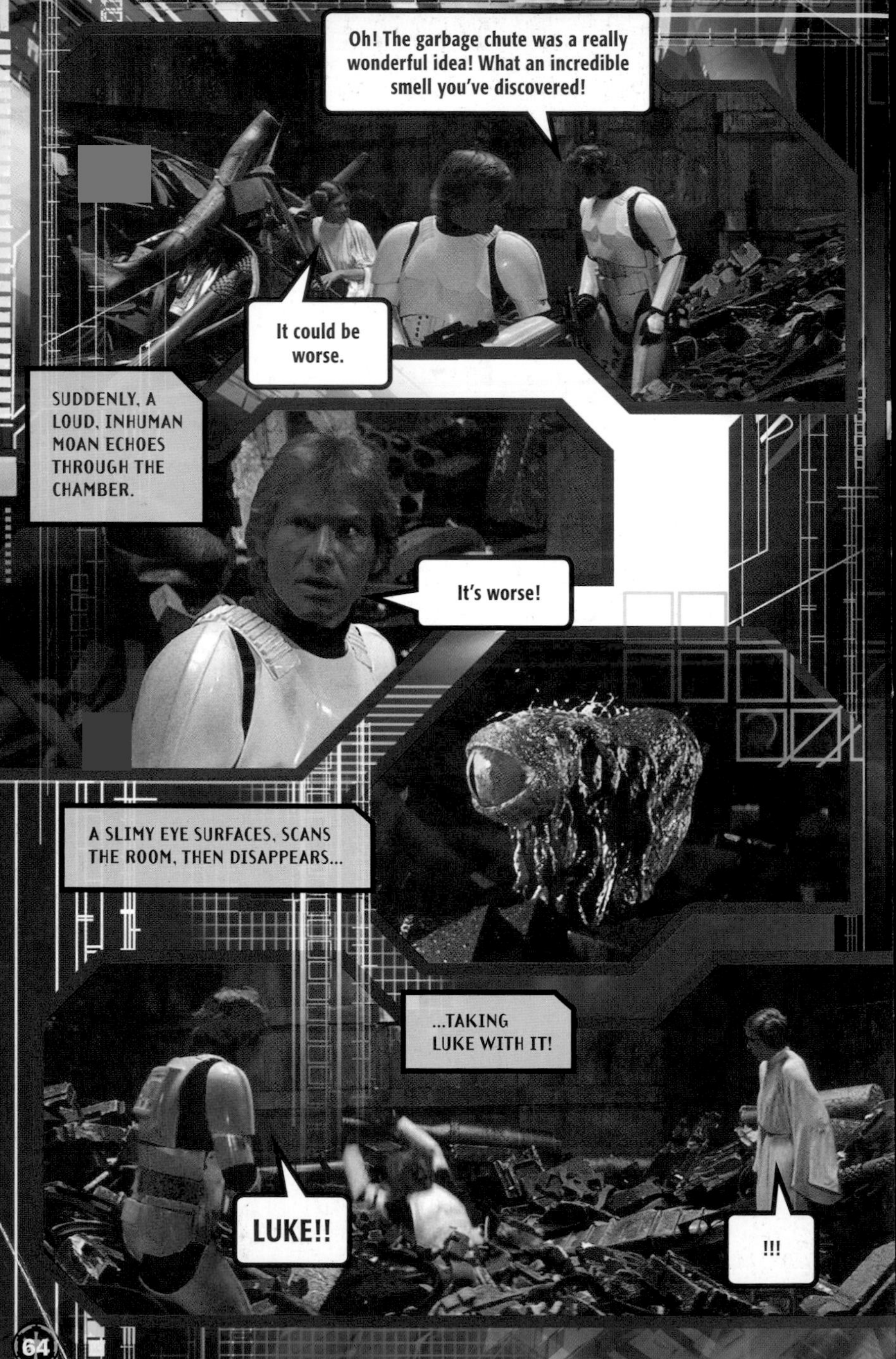
Oh! The garbage chute was a really wonderful idea! What an incredible smell you've discovered!
It could be worse.
SUDDENLY, A LOUD, INHUMAN MOAN ECHOES THROUGH THE CHAMBER.
It's worse!
A SLIMY EYE SURFACES, SCANS THE ROOM, THEN DISAPPEARS...
...TAKING LUKE WITH IT!
LUKE!!
!!!

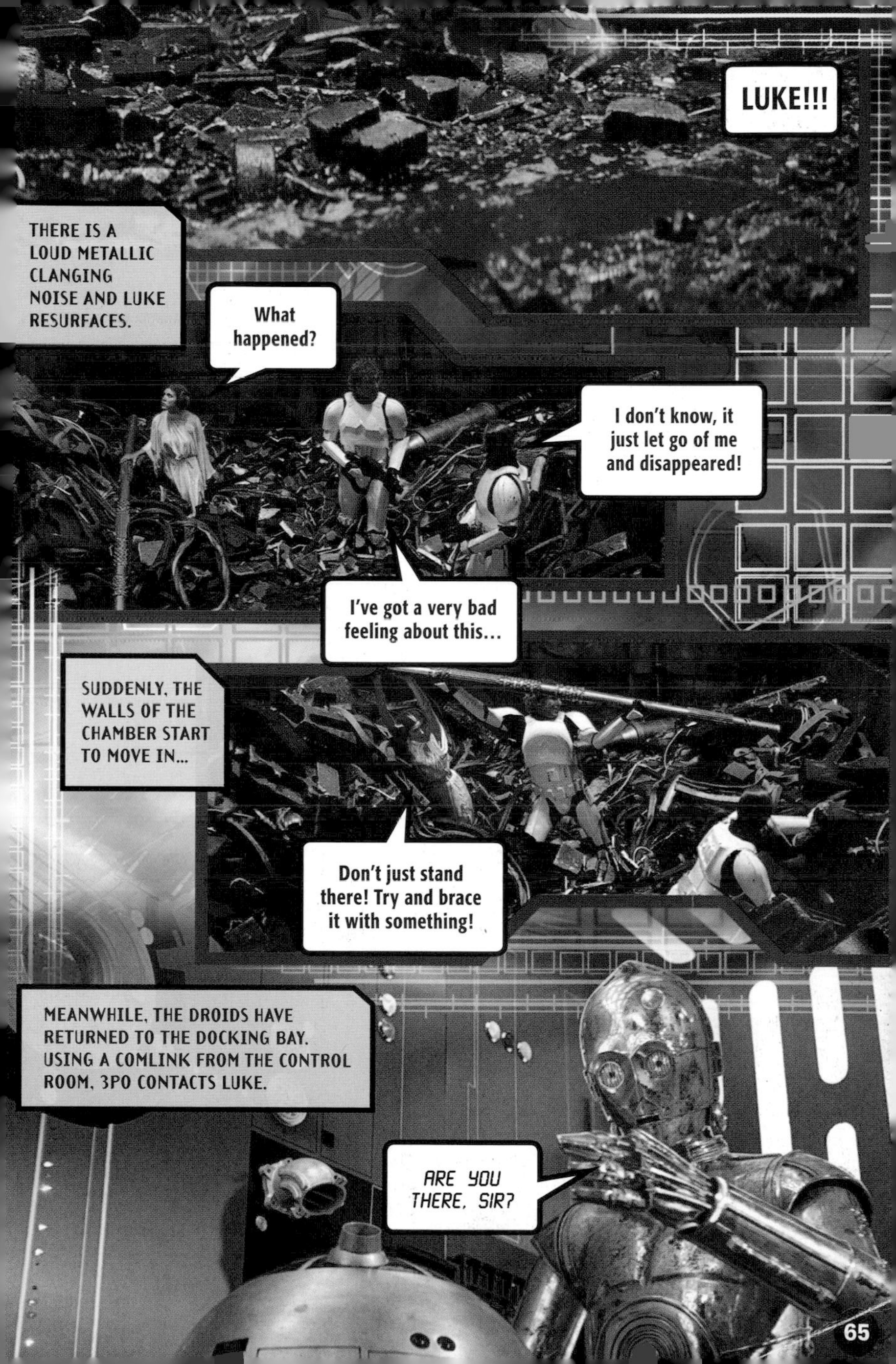
LUKE!!!
THERE IS A LOUD METALLIC CLANGING NOISE AND LUKE RESURFACES.
What happened?
I don't know, it just let go of me and disappeared!
I've got a very bad feeling about this...
SUDDENLY, THE WALLS OF THE CHAMBER START TO MOVE IN...
Don't just stand there! Try and brace it with something!
MEANWHILE, THE DROIDS HAVE RETURNED TO THE DOCKING BAY. USING A COMLINK FROM THE CONTROL ROOM, 3PO CONTACTS LUKE.
ARE YOU THERE, SIR?

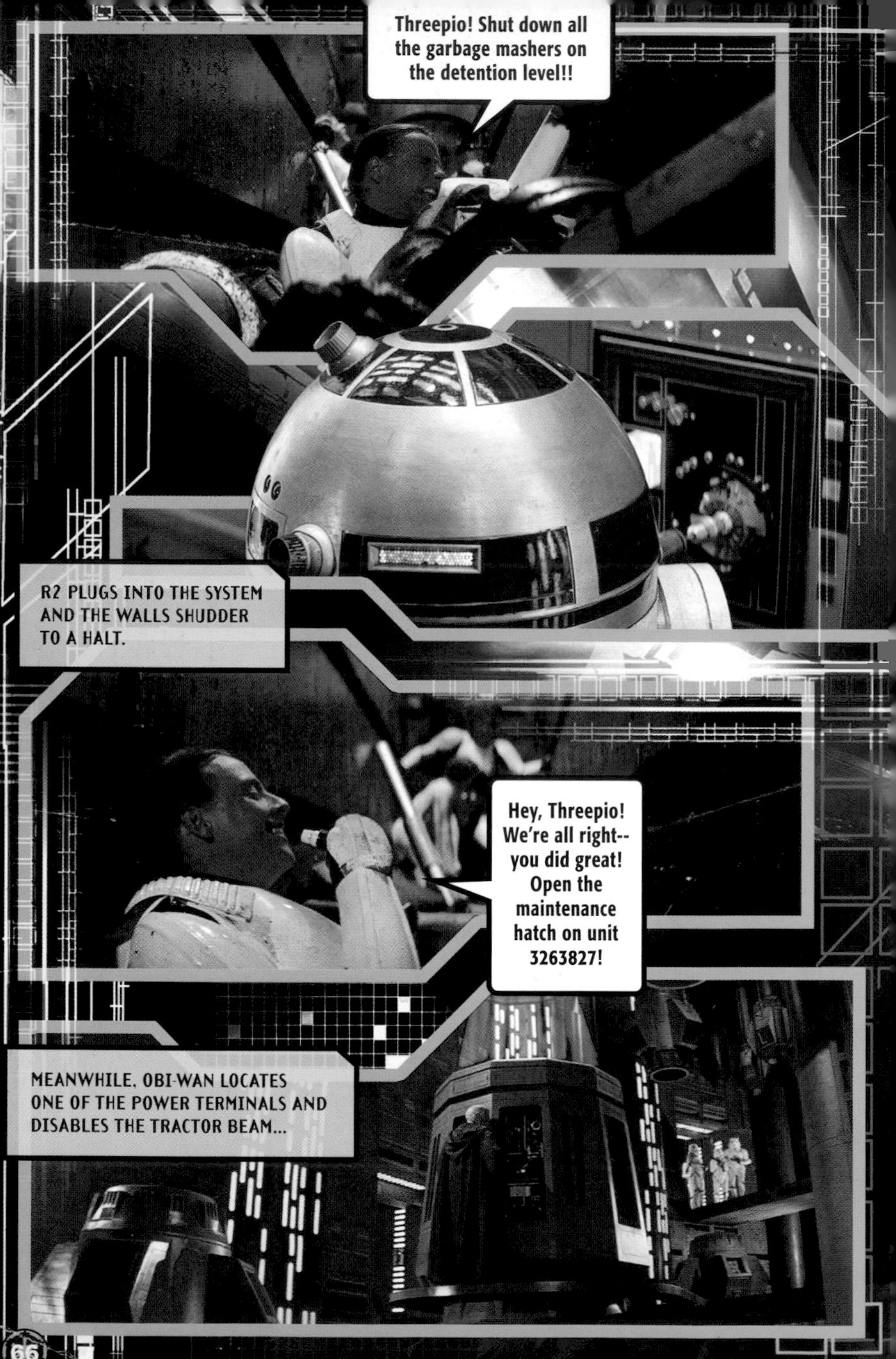
Threepio! Shut down all the garbage mashers on the detention level!!
R2 PLUGS INTO THE SYSTEM AND THE WALLS SHUDDER TO A HALT.
Hey, Threepio! We're all right-- you did great! Open the maintenance hatch on unit 3263827!
MEANWHILE, OBI-WAN LOCATES ONE OF THE POWER TERMINALS AND DISABLES THE TRACTOR BEAM...

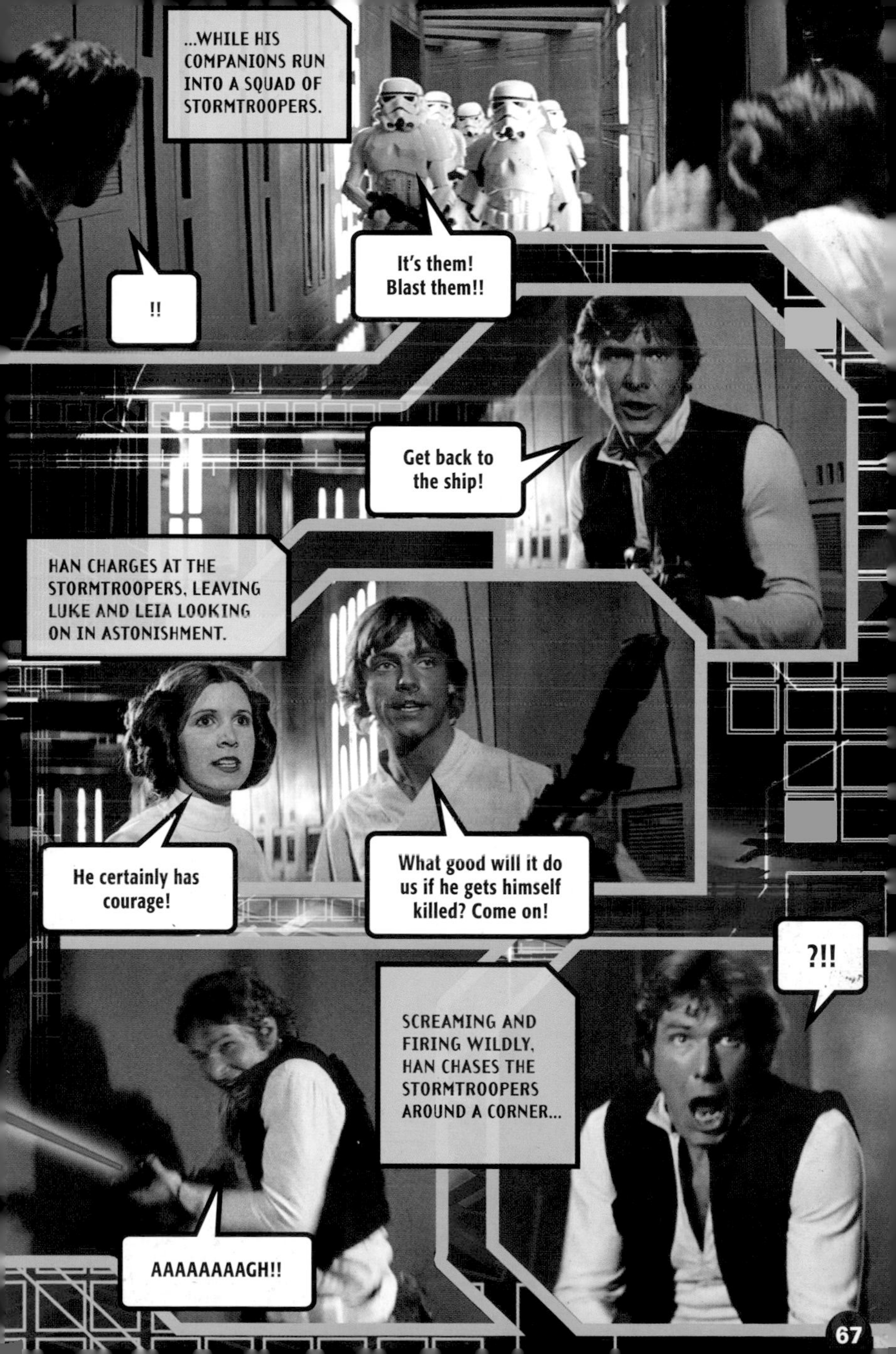
...WHILE HIS COMPANIONS RUN INTO A SQUAD OF STORMTROOPERS.
!!
It's them! Blast them!!
Get back to the ship!
HAN CHARGES AT THE STORMTROOPERS, LEAVING LUKE AND LEIA LOOKING ON IN ASTONISHMENT.
He certainly has courage!
What good will it do us if he gets himself killed? Come on!
AAAAAAAAGH!!
SCREAMING AND FIRING WILDLY, HAN CHASES THE STORMTROOPERS AROUND A CORNER...
?!!

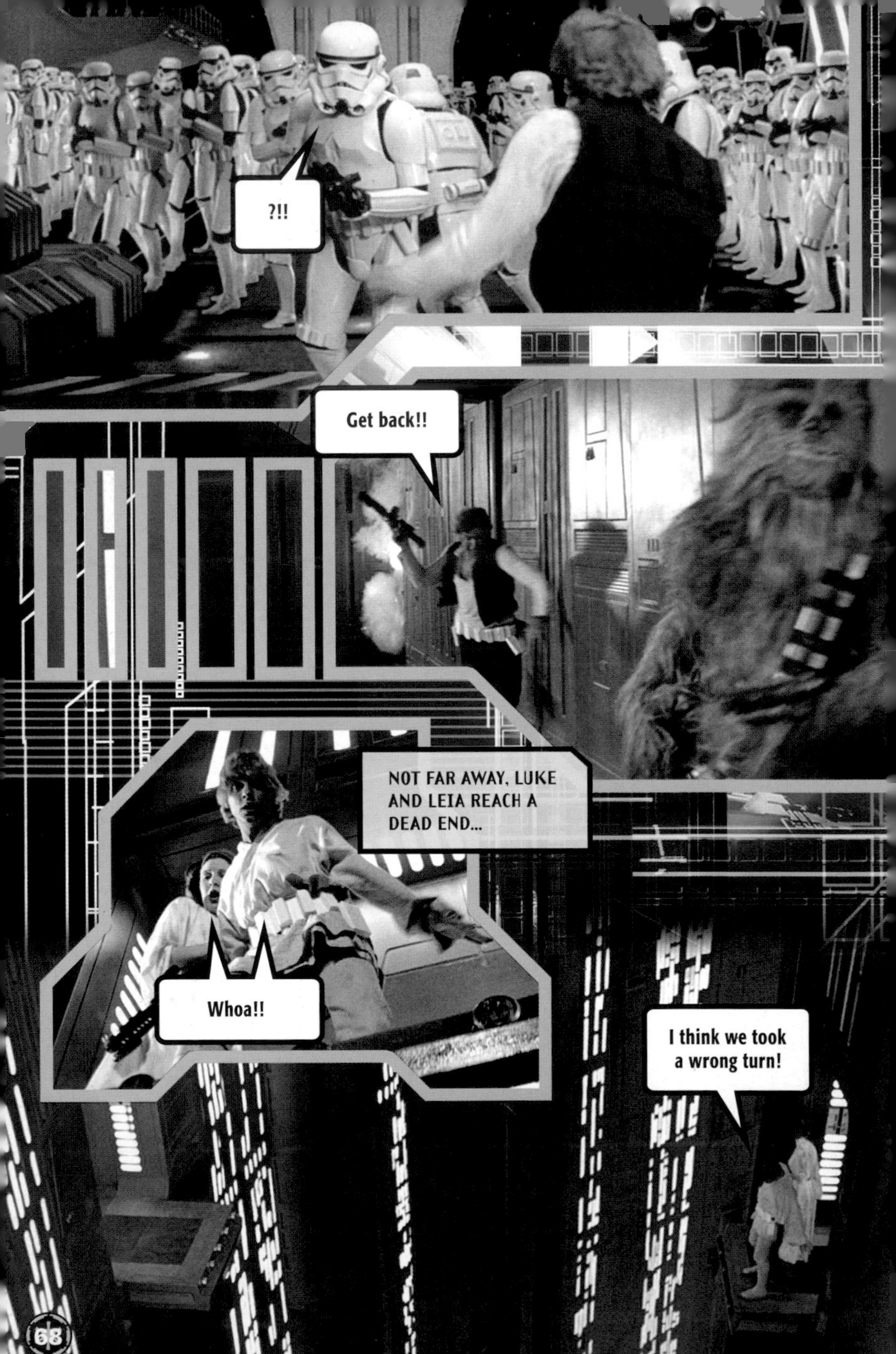
?!!
Get back!!
NOT FAR AWAY, LUKE AND LEIA REACH A DEAD END...
Whoa!!
I think we took a wrong turn!

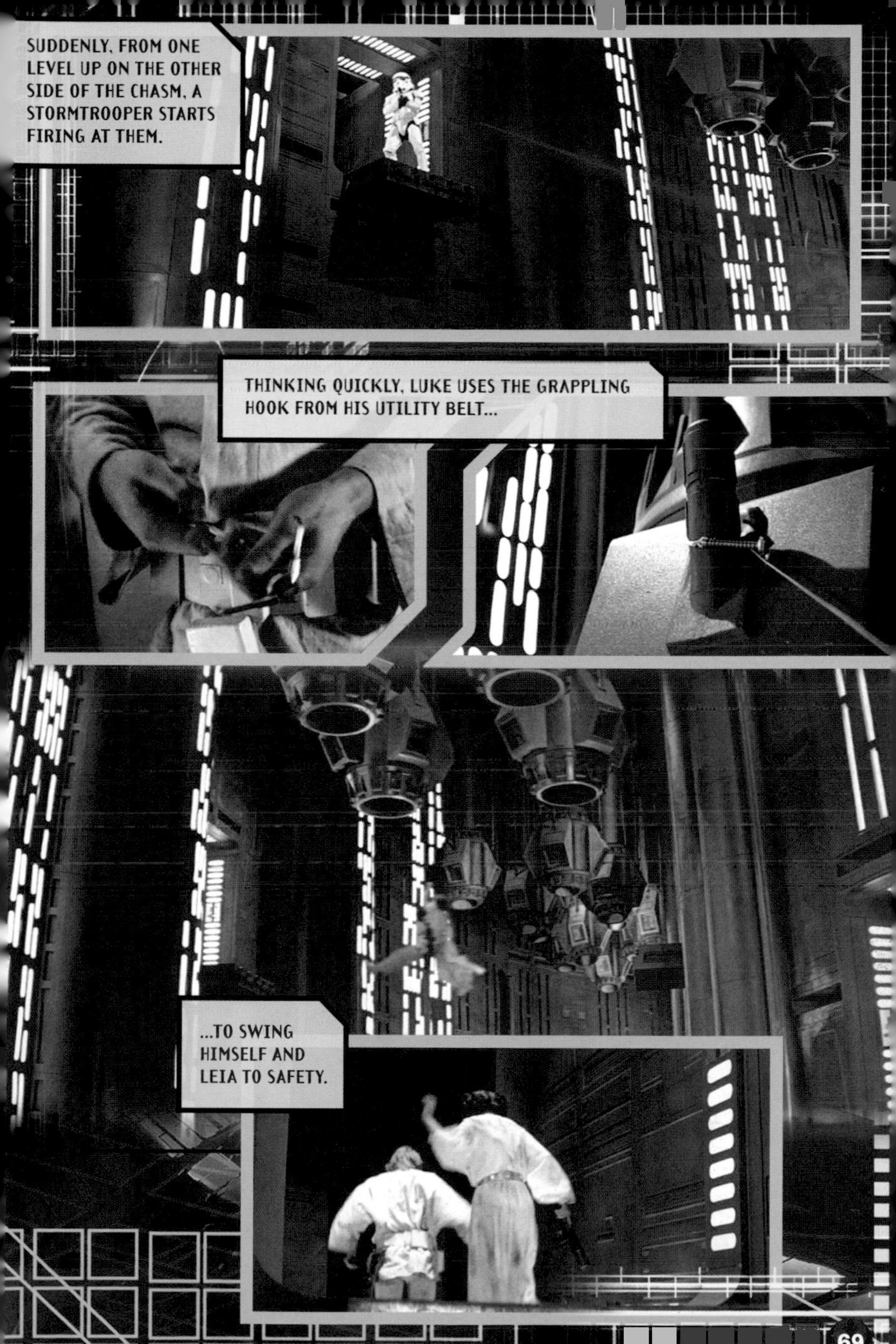
SUDDENLY, FROM ONE LEVEL UP ON THE OTHER SIDE OF THE CHASM, A STORMTROOPER STARTS FIRING AT THEM.
THINKING QUICKLY, LUKE USES THE GRAPPLING HOOK FROM HIS UTILITY BELT...
...TO SWING HIMSELF AND LEIA TO SAFETY.

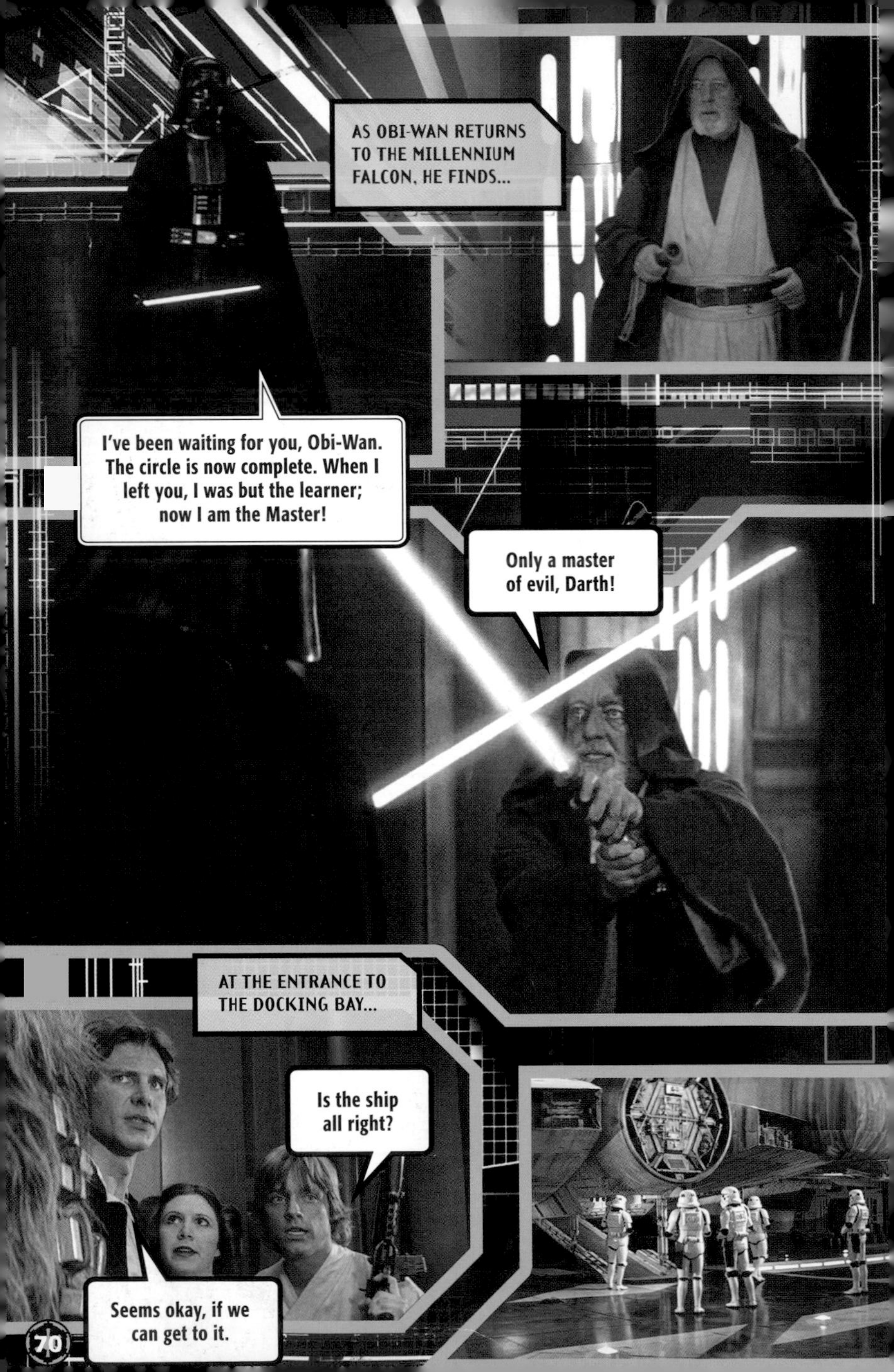
AS OBI-WAN RETURNS TO THE MILLENNIUM FALCON, HE FINDS...
I've been waiting for you, Obi-Wan. The circle is now complete. When I left you, I was but the learner; now I am the Master!
Only a master of evil, Darth!
AT THE ENTRANCE TO THE DOCKING BAY...
Is the ship all right?
Seems okay, if we can get to it.

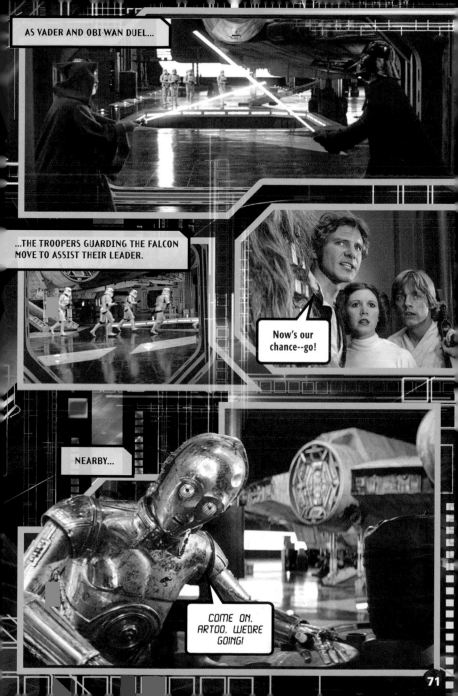

AS VADER AND OBI-WAN DUEL...

...THE TROOPERS GUARDING THE FALCON MOVE TO ASSIST THEIR LEADER.

Now's our chance--go!

NEARBY...

COME ON, ARTOO, WE'RE GOING!

71

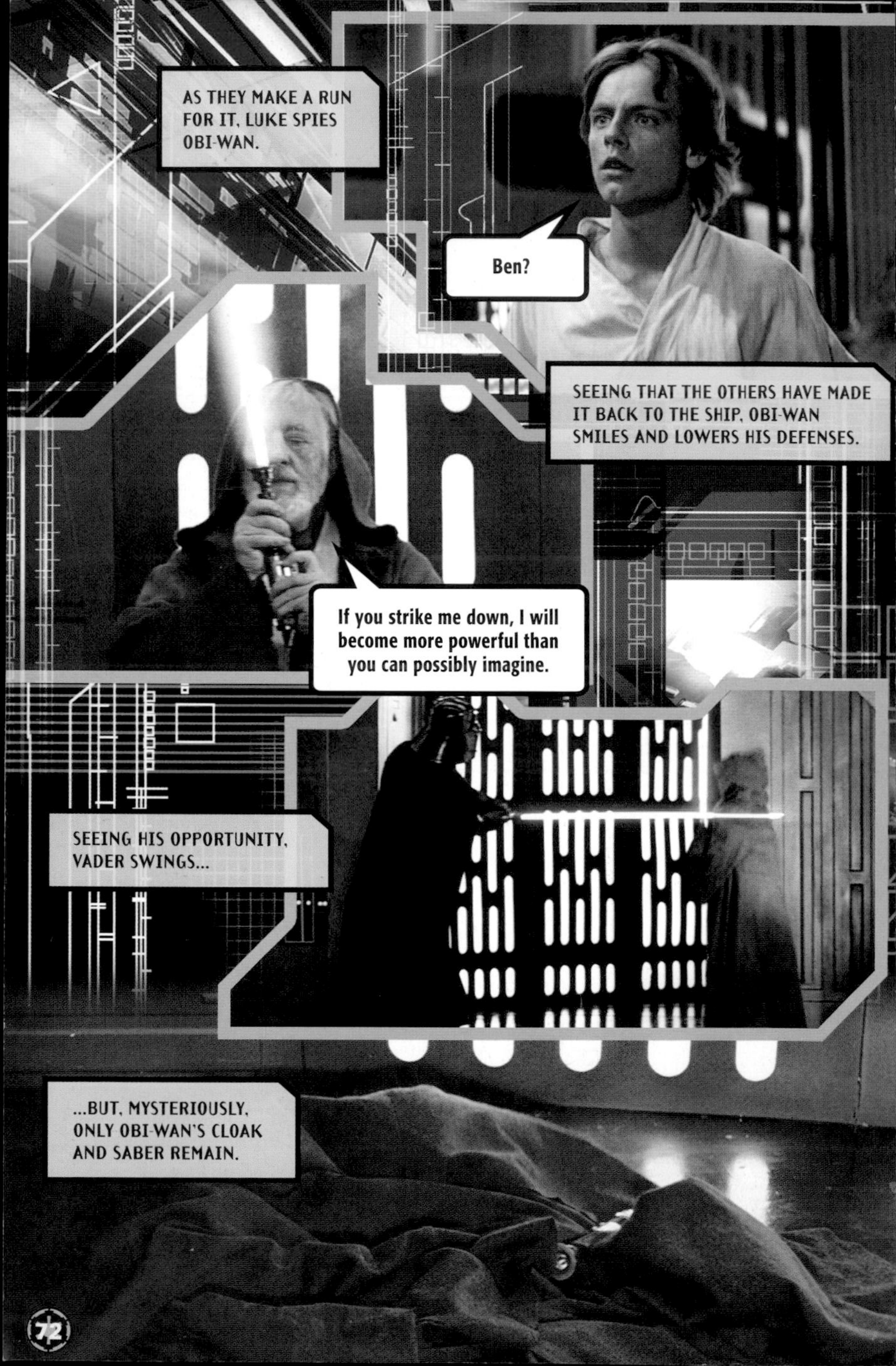
AS THEY MAKE A RUN FOR IT, LUKE SPIES OBI-WAN.
Ben?
SEEING THAT THE OTHERS HAVE MADE IT BACK TO THE SHIP, OBI-WAN SMILES AND LOWERS HIS DEFENSES.
If you strike me down, I will become more powerful than you can possibly imagine.
SEEING HIS OPPORTUNITY, VADER SWINGS...
...BUT, MYSTERIOUSLY, ONLY OBI-WAN'S CLOAK AND SABER REMAIN.

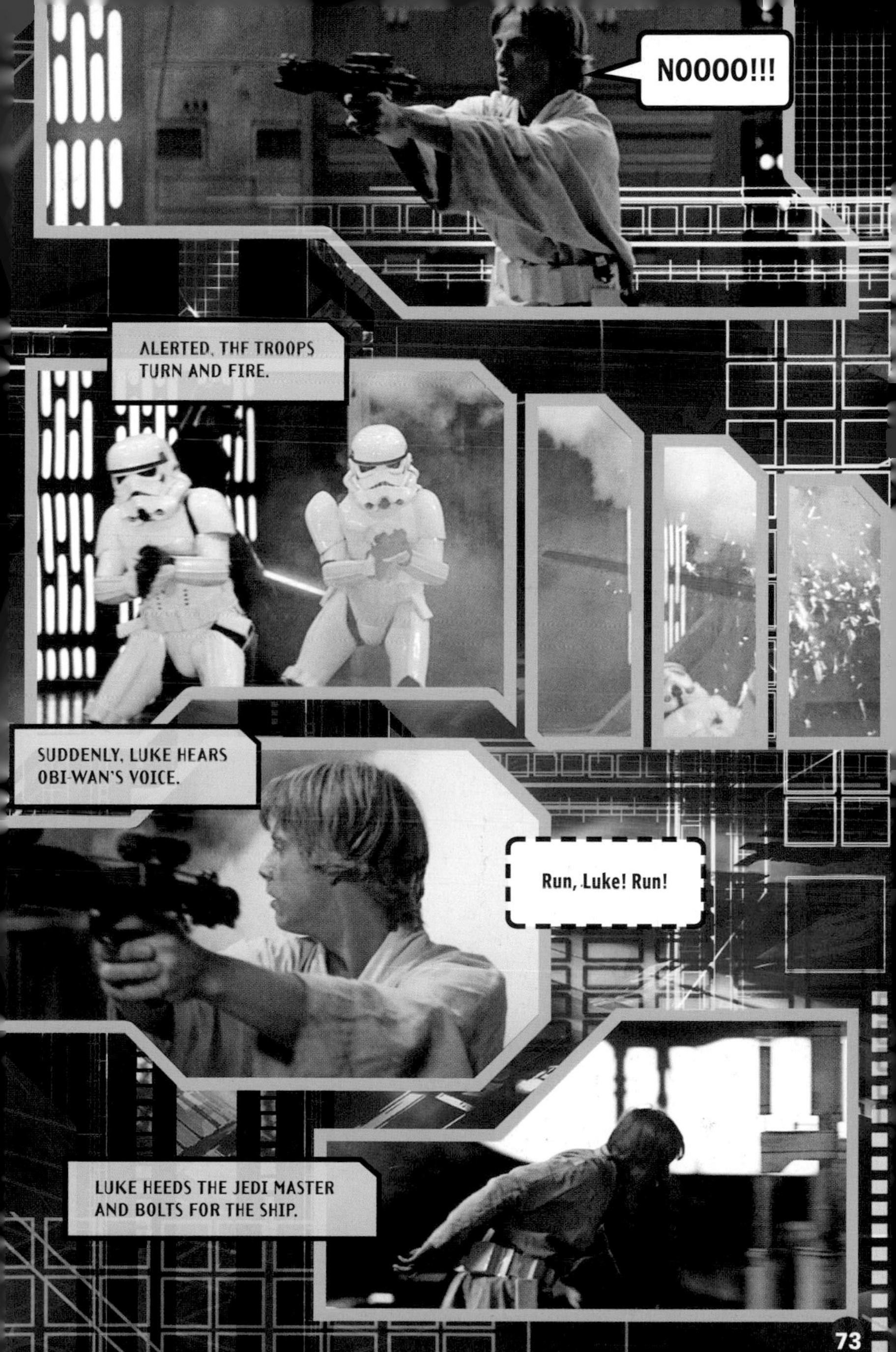
NOOOO!!!
ALERTED, THE TROOPS TURN AND FIRE.
SUDDENLY, LUKE HEARS OBI-WAN'S VOICE.
Run, Luke! Run!
LUKE HEEDS THE JEDI MASTER AND BOLTS FOR THE SHIP.

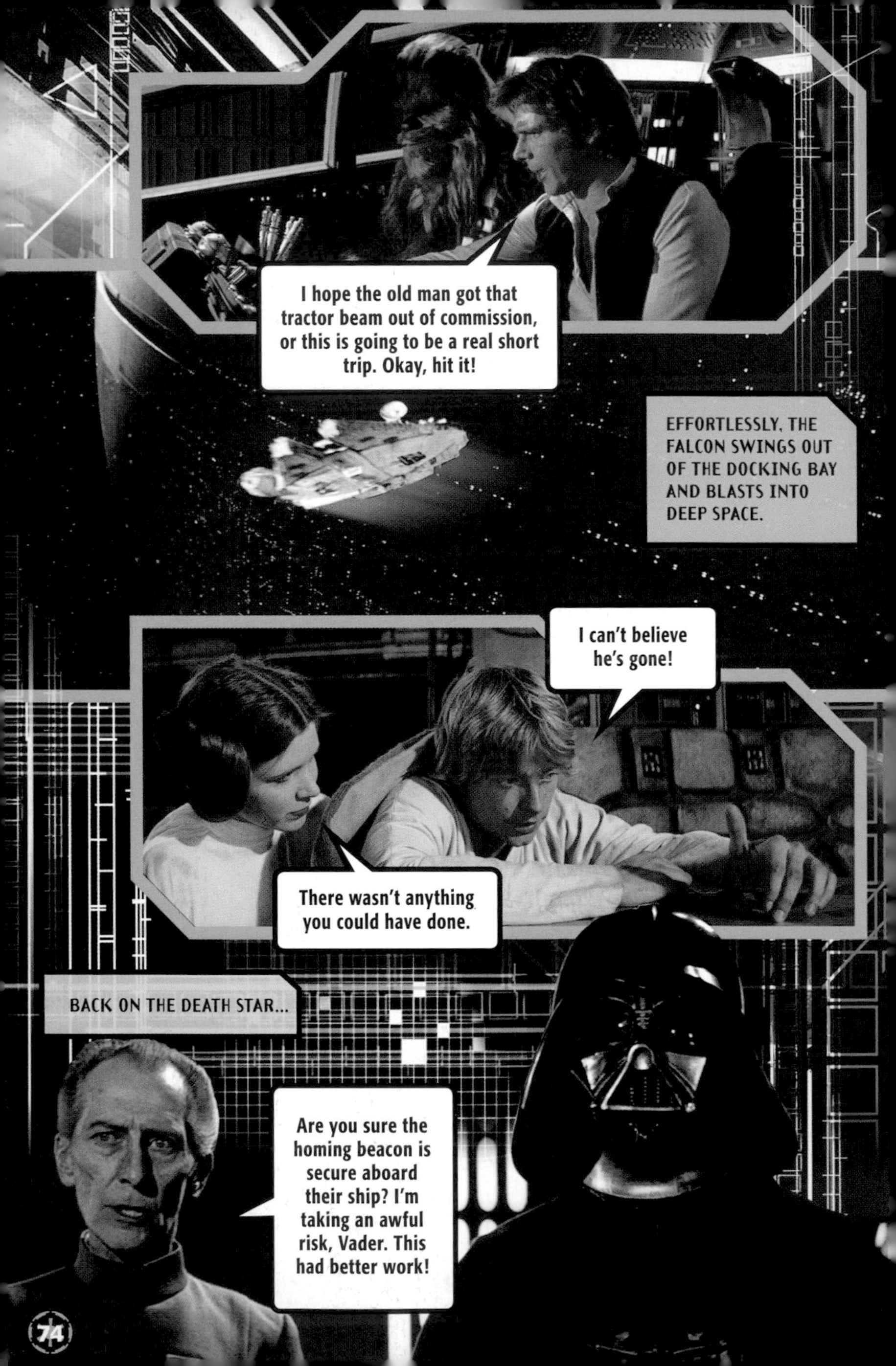
I hope the old man got that tractor beam out of commission, or this is going to be a real short trip. Okay, hit it!
EFFORTLESSLY, THE FALCON SWINGS OUT OF THE DOCKING BAY AND BLASTS INTO DEEP SPACE.
I can't believe he's gone!
There wasn't anything you could have done.
BACK ON THE DEATH STAR...
Are you sure the homing beacon is secure aboard their ship? I'm taking an awful risk, Vader. This had better work!

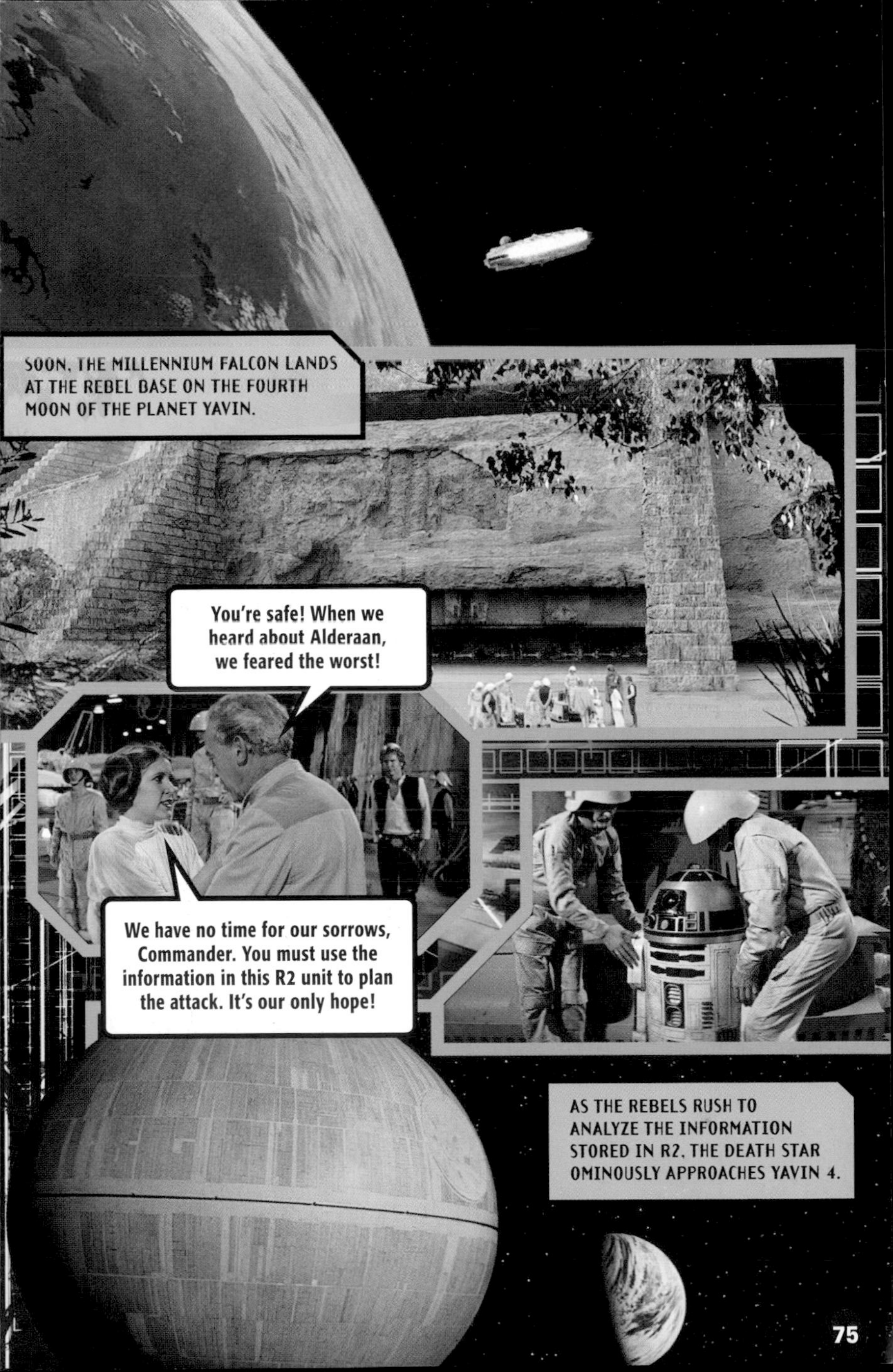
SOON, THE MILLENNIUM FALCON LANDS AT THE REBEL BASE ON THE FOURTH MOON OF THE PLANET YAVIN.
You're safe! When we heard about Alderaan, we feared the worst!
We have no time for our sorrows, Commander. You must use the information in this R2 unit to plan the attack. It's our only hope!
AS THE REBELS RUSH TO ANALYZE THE INFORMATION STORED IN R2, THE DEATH STAR OMINOUSLY APPROACHES YAVIN 4.

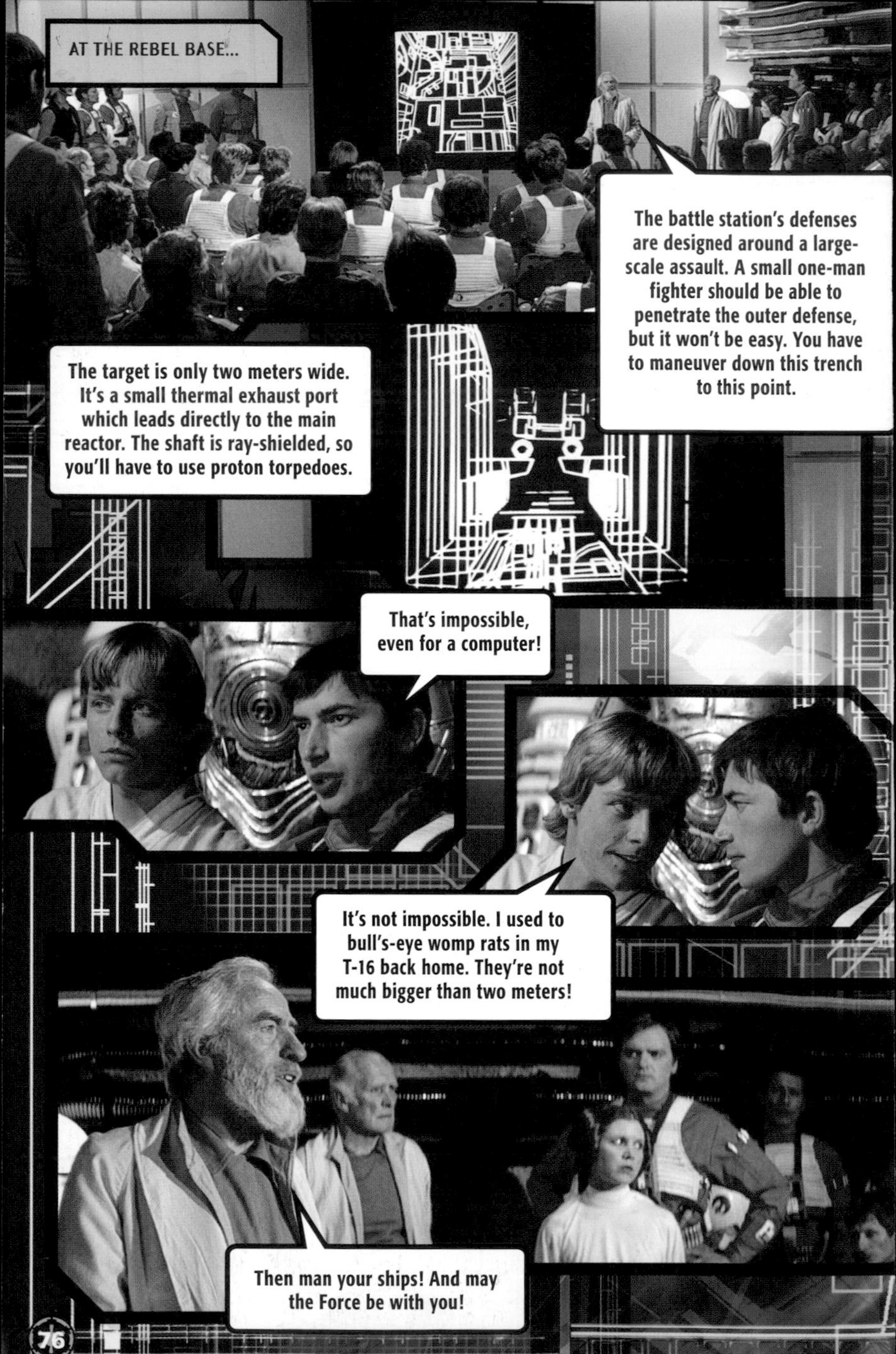
AT THE REBEL BASE...
The battle station's defenses are designed around a large-scale assault. A small one-man fighter should be able to penetrate the outer defense, but it won't be easy. You have to maneuver down this trench to this point.
The target is only two meters wide. It's a small thermal exhaust port which leads directly to the main reactor. The shaft is ray-shielded, so you'll have to use proton torpedoes.
That's impossible, even for a computer!
It's not impossible. I used to bull's-eye womp rats in my T-16 back home. They're not much bigger than two meters!
Then man your ships! And may the Force be with you!

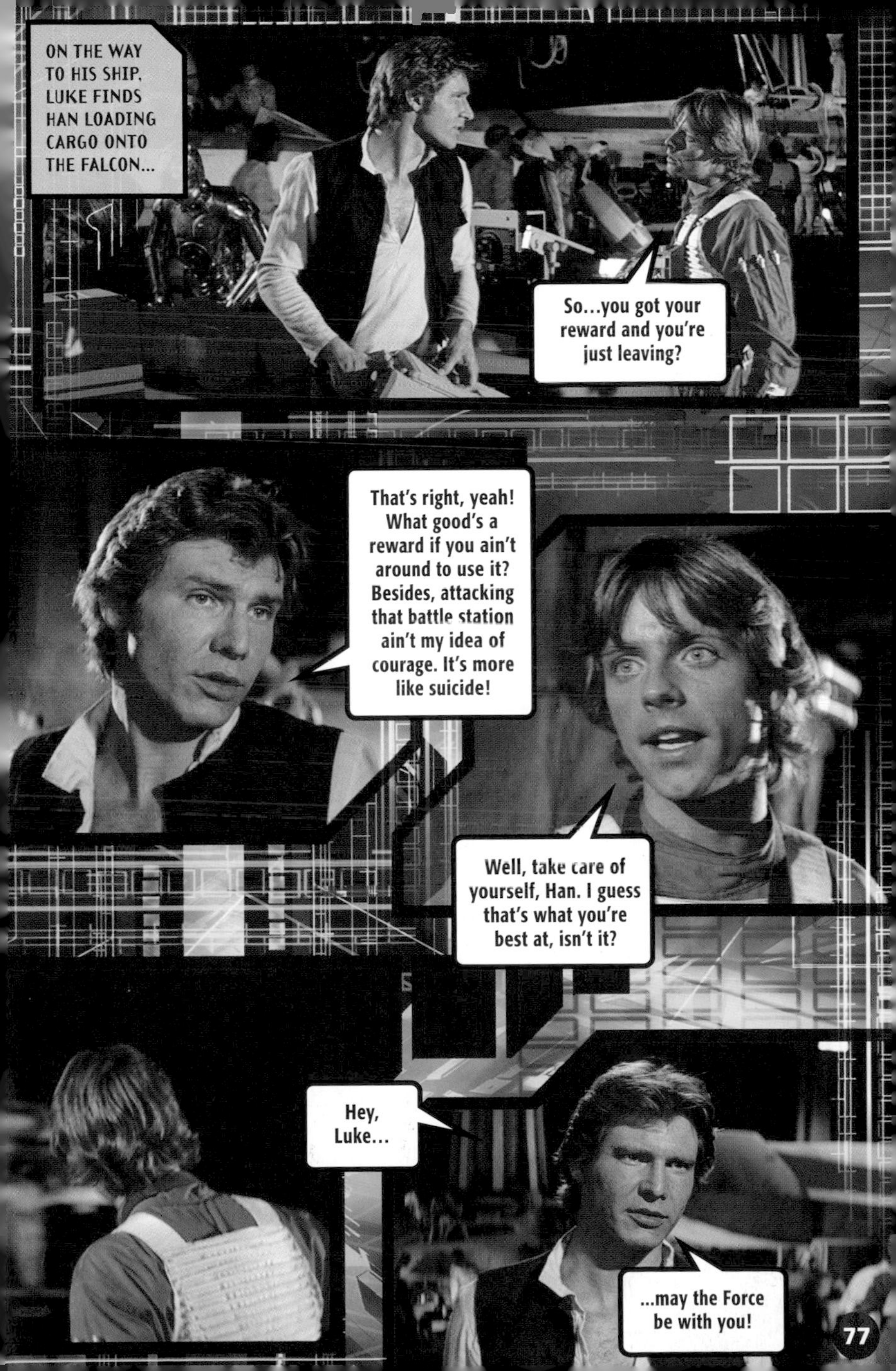

ON THE WAY TO HIS SHIP, LUKE FINDS HAN LOADING CARGO ONTO THE FALCON...
So...you got your reward and you're just leaving?
That's right, yeah! What good's a reward if you ain't around to use it? Besides, attacking that battle station ain't my idea of courage. It's more like suicide!
Well, take care of yourself, Han. I guess that's what you're best at, isn't it?
Hey, Luke...
...may the Force be with you!

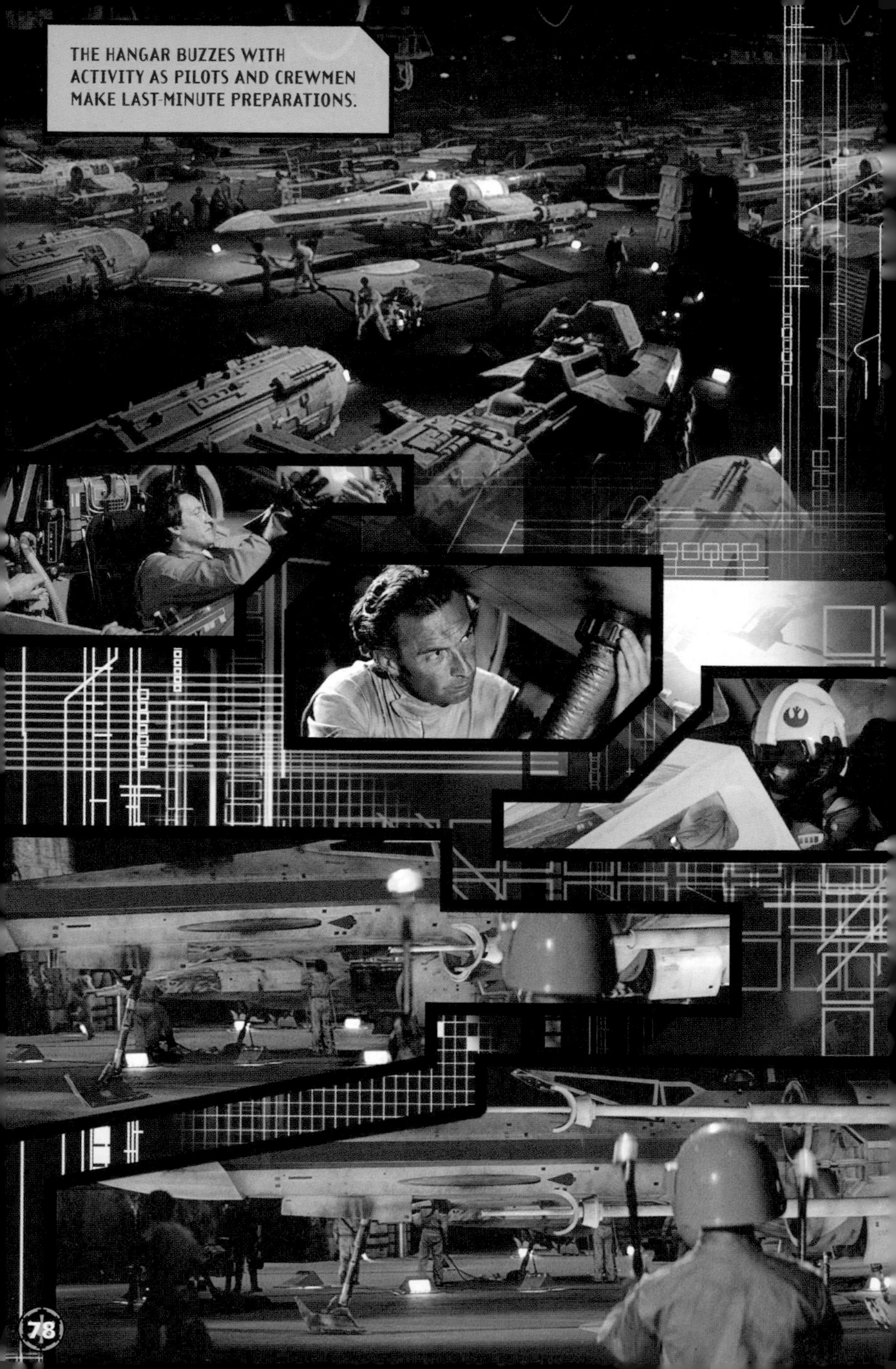
THE HANGAR BUZZES WITH ACTIVITY AS PILOTS AND CREWMEN MAKE LAST-MINUTE PREPARATIONS.

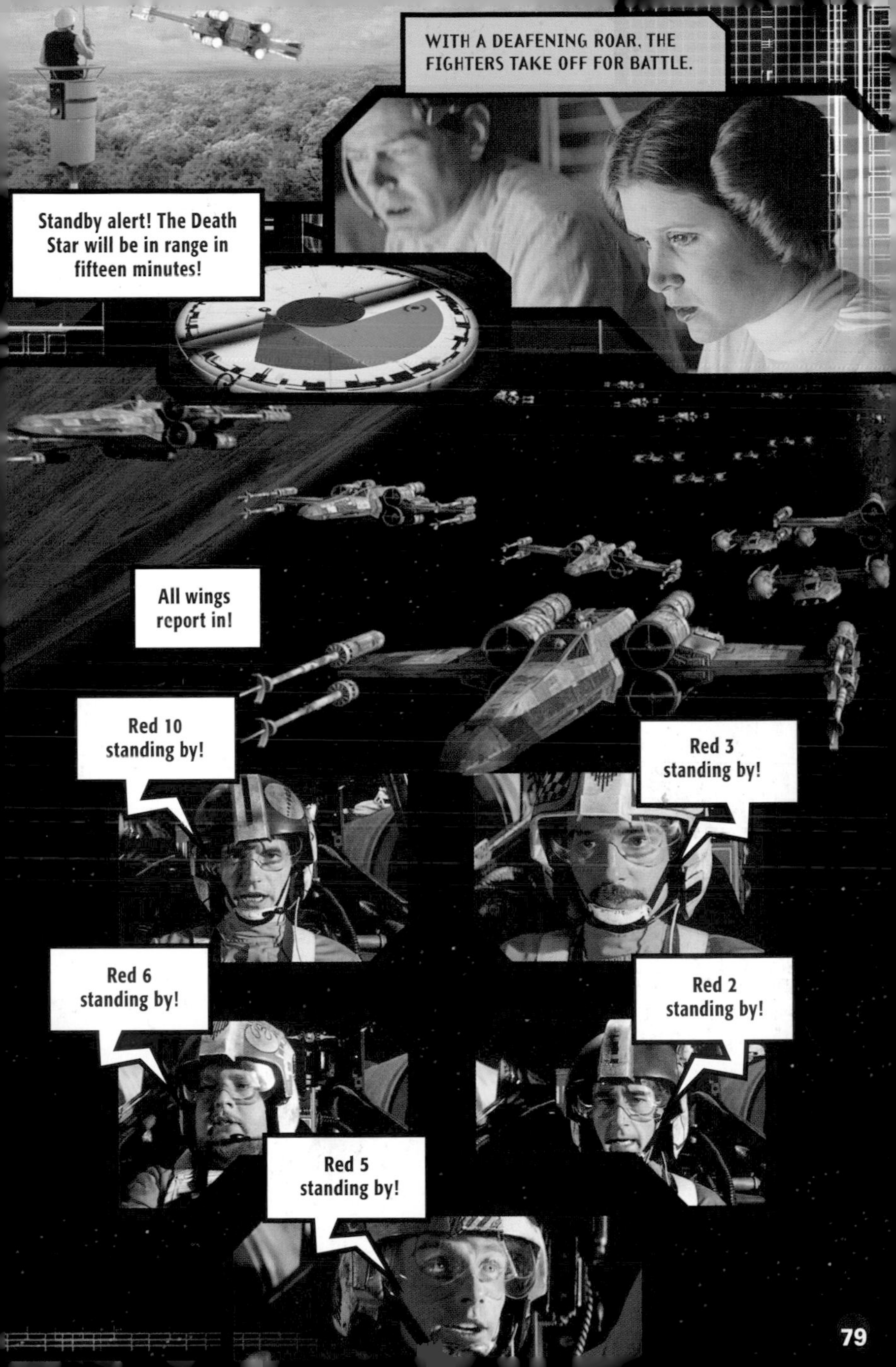
WITH A DEAFENING ROAR, THE FIGHTERS TAKE OFF FOR BATTLE.
Standby alert! The Death Star will be in range in fifteen minutes!
All wings report in!
Red 10 standing by!
Red 3 standing by!
Red 6 standing by!
Red 2 standing by!
Red 5 standing by!

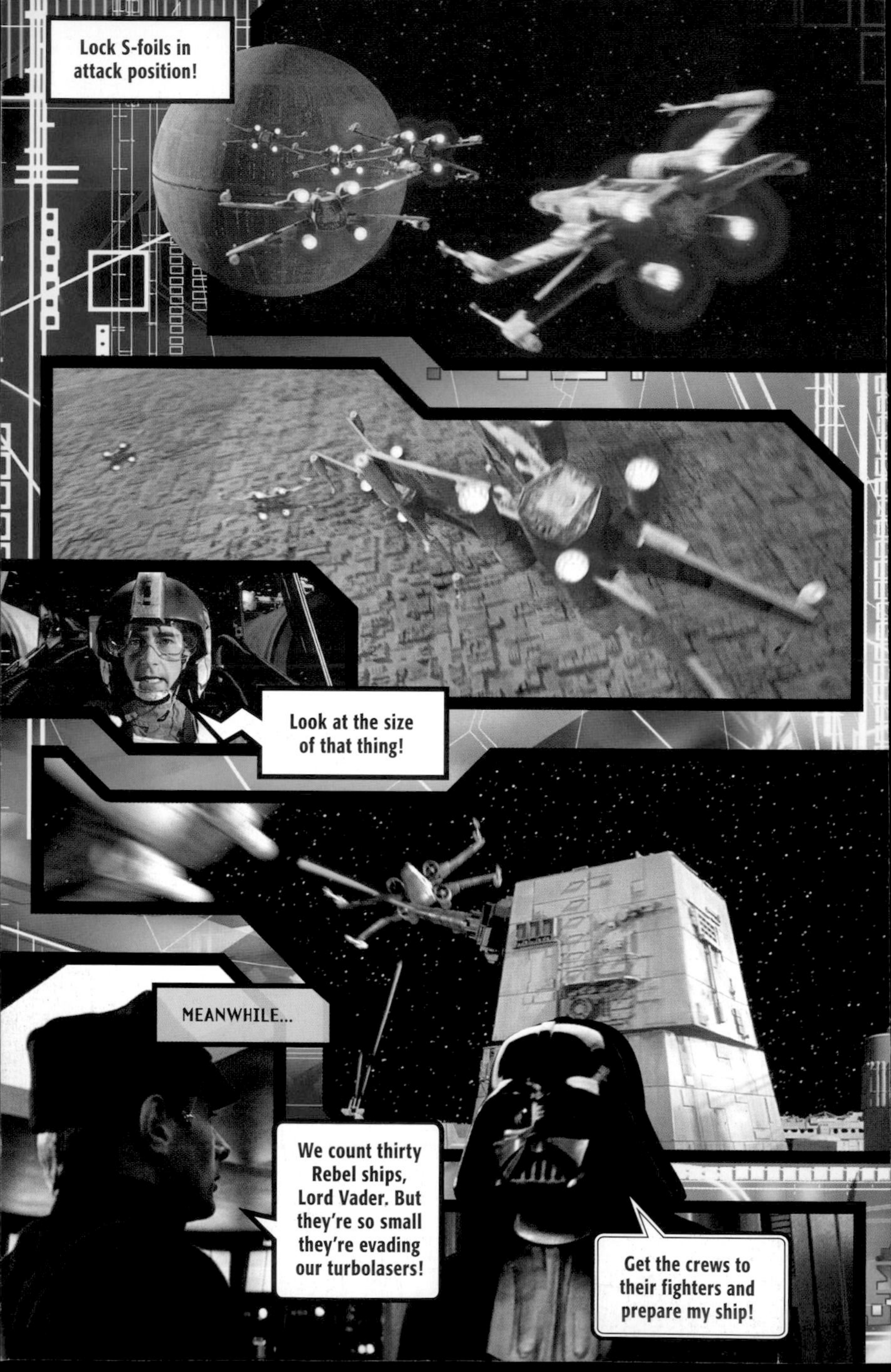
Lock S-foils in attack position!
Look at the size of that thing!
MEANWHILE...
We count thirty Rebel ships, Lord Vader. But they're so small they're evading our turbolasers!
Get the crews to their fighters and prepare my ship!

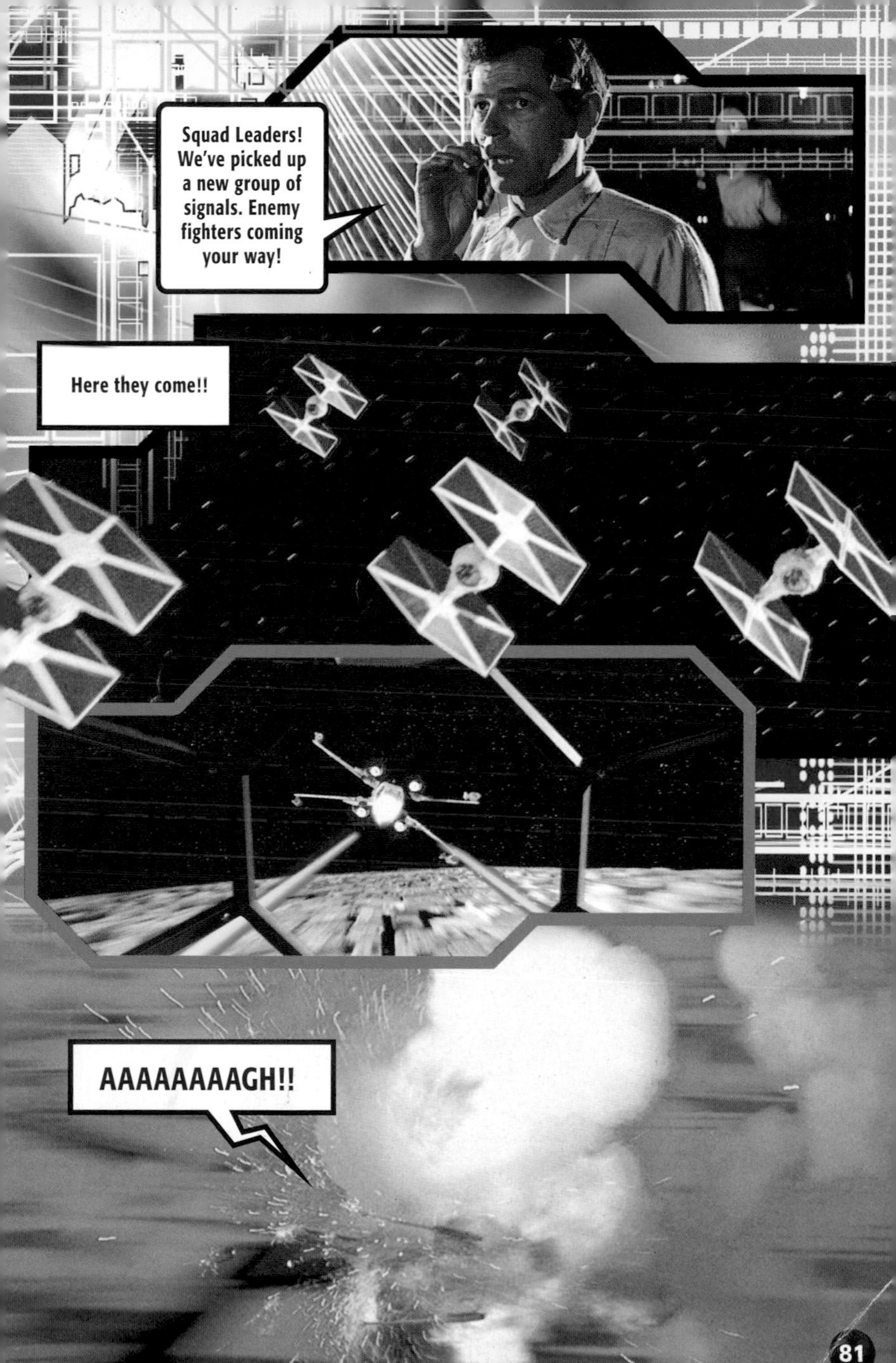
Squad Leaders! We've picked up a new group of signals. Enemy fighters coming your way!
Here they come!!
AAAAAAAAGH!!

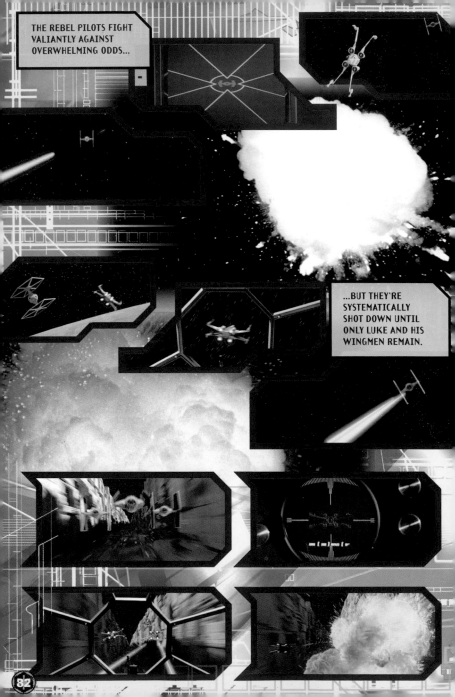

THE REBEL PILOTS FIGHT VALIANTLY AGAINST OVERWHELMING ODDS...

...BUT THEY'RE SYSTEMATICALLY SHOT DOWN UNTIL ONLY LUKE AND HIS WINGMEN REMAIN.

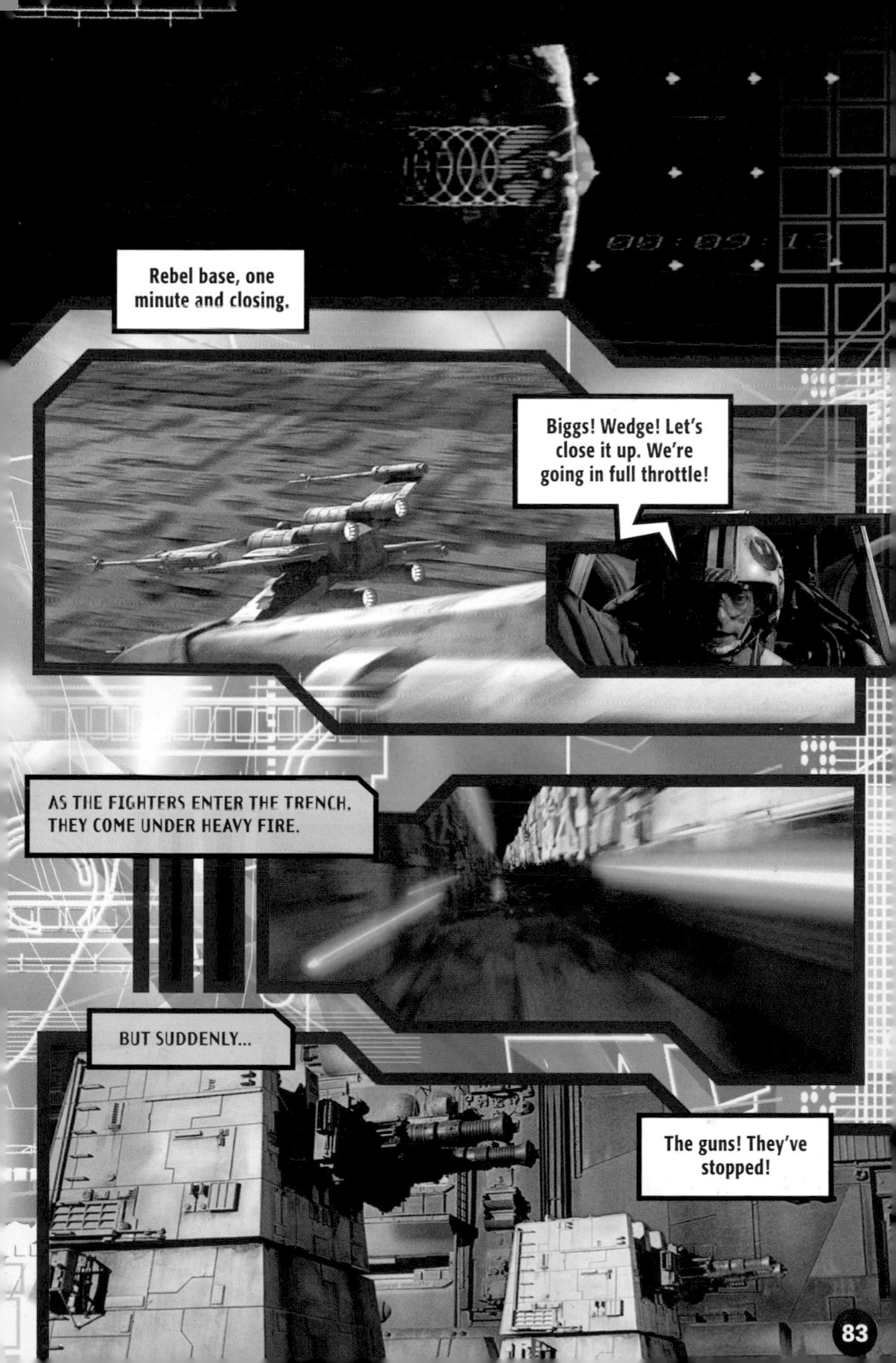
Rebel base, one minute and closing.
Biggs! Wedge! Let's close it up. We're going in full throttle!
AS THE FIGHTERS ENTER THE TRENCH, THEY COME UNDER HEAVY FIRE.
BUT SUDDENLY...
The guns! They've stopped!

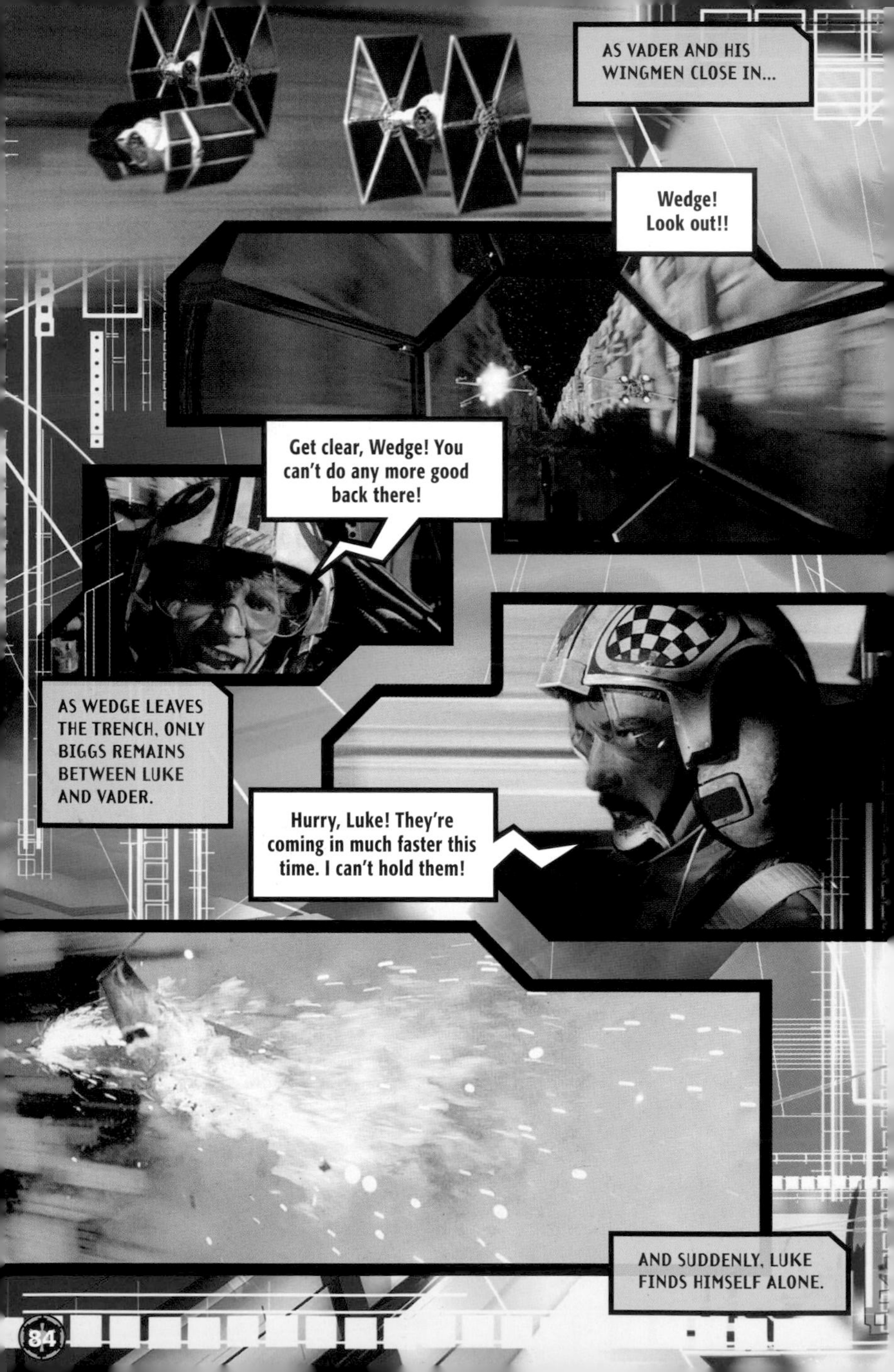
AS VADER AND HIS WINGMEN CLOSE IN...
Wedge! Look out!!
Get clear, Wedge! You can't do any more good back there!
AS WEDGE LEAVES THE TRENCH, ONLY BIGGS REMAINS BETWEEN LUKE AND VADER.
Hurry, Luke! They're coming in much faster this time. I can't hold them!
AND SUDDENLY, LUKE FINDS HIMSELF ALONE.

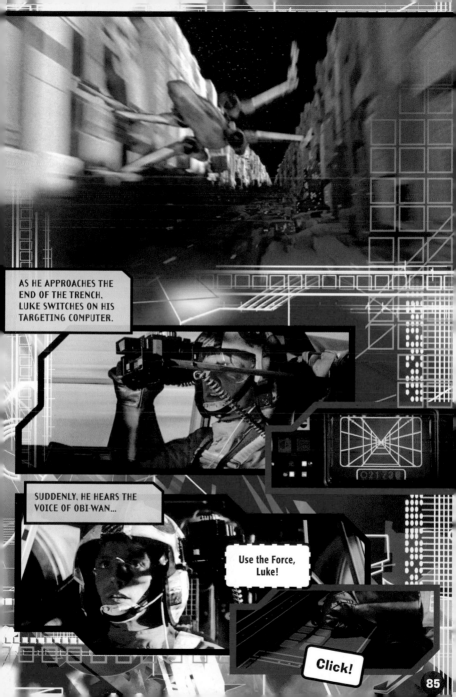

AS HE APPROACHES THE END OF THE TRENCH, LUKE SWITCHES ON HIS TARGETING COMPUTER.

SUDDENLY, HE HEARS THE VOICE OF OBI-WAN...

Use the Force, Luke!

Click!

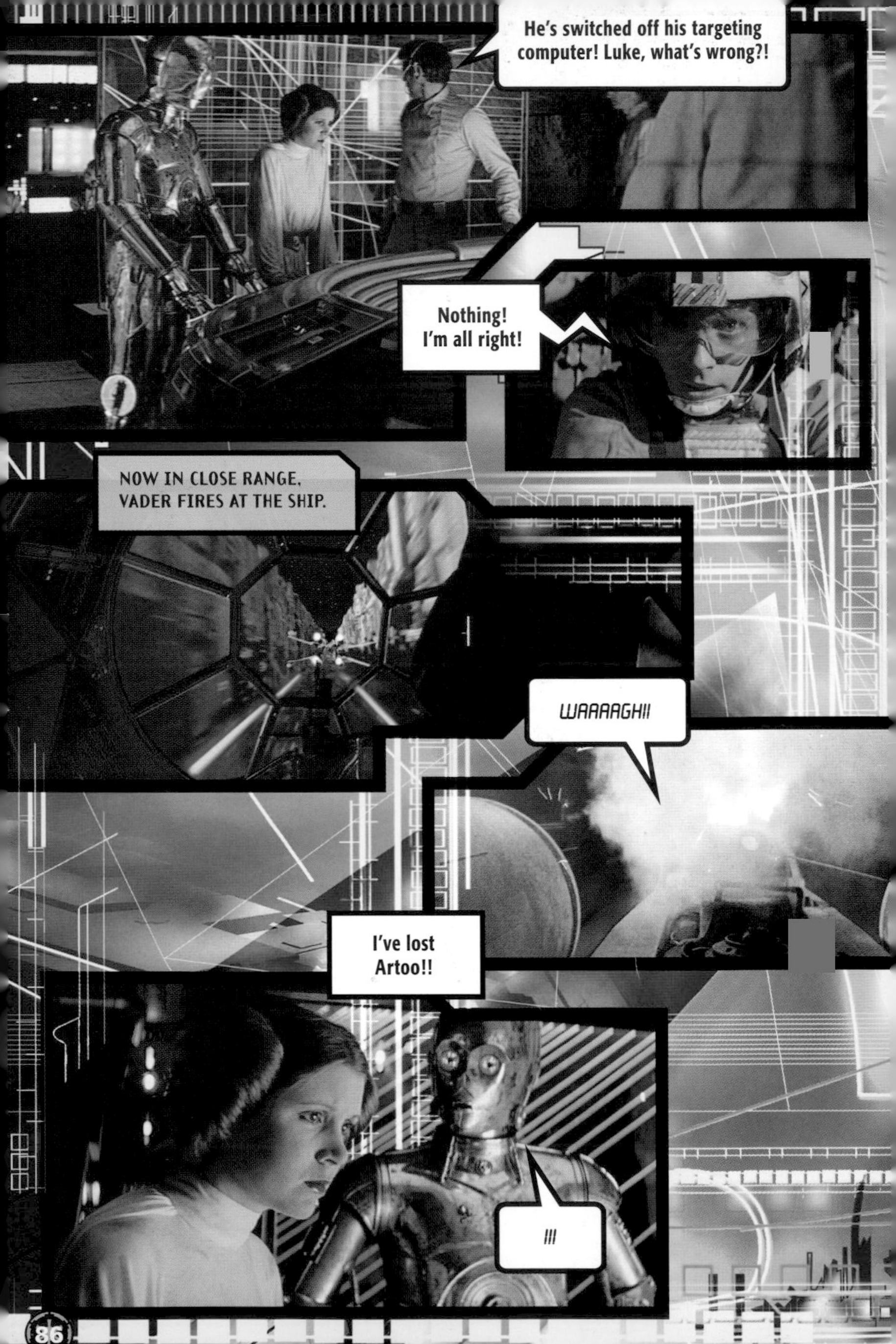
He's switched off his targeting computer! Luke, what's wrong?!
Nothing! I'm all right!
NOW IN CLOSE RANGE, VADER FIRES AT THE SHIP.
WAAAAGH!!
I've lost Artoo!!
!!!

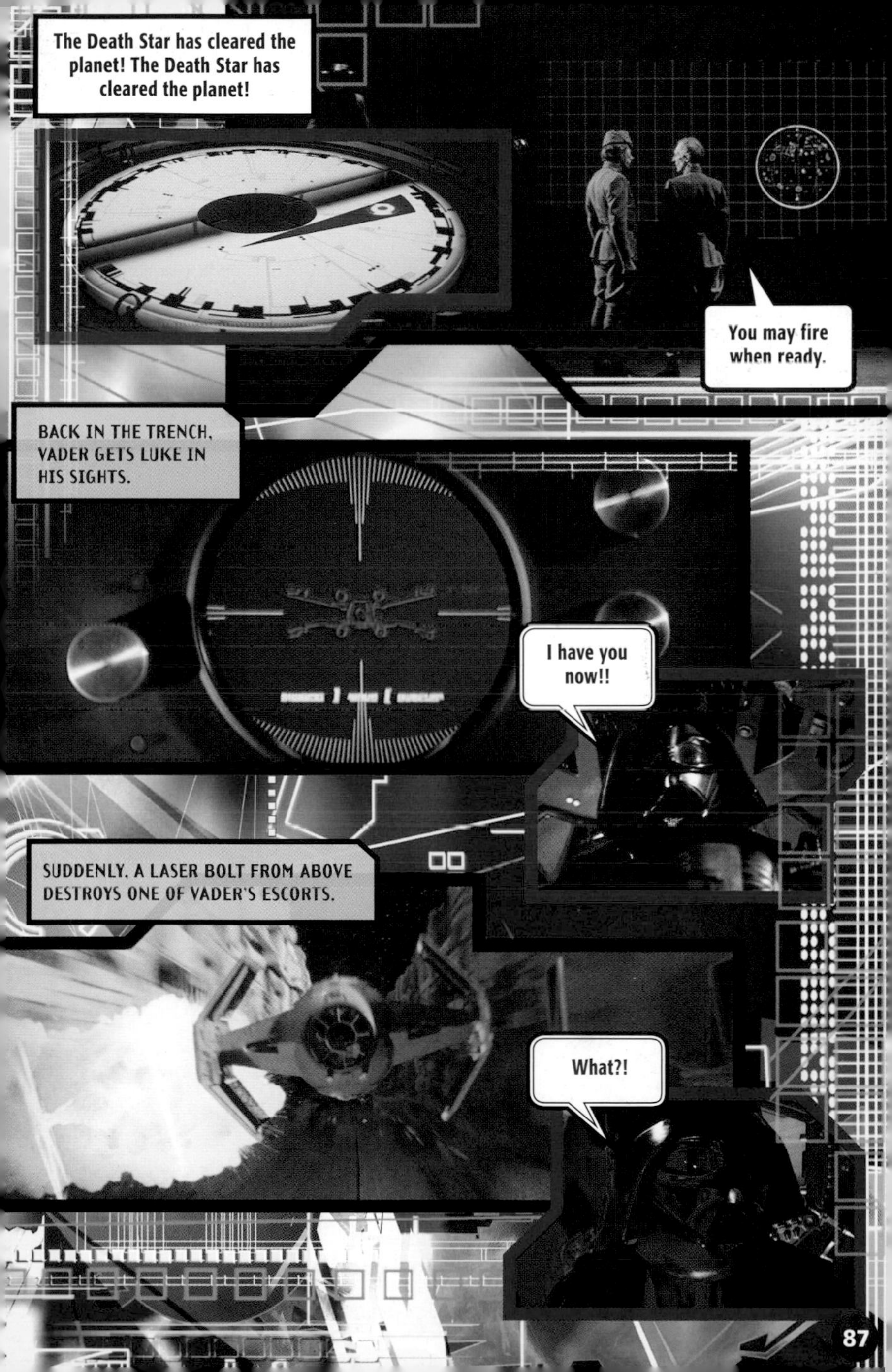
The Death Star has cleared the planet! The Death Star has cleared the planet!
You may fire when ready.
BACK IN THE TRENCH, VADER GETS LUKE IN HIS SIGHTS.
I have you now!!
SUDDENLY, A LASER BOLT FROM ABOVE DESTROYS ONE OF VADER'S ESCORTS.
What?!

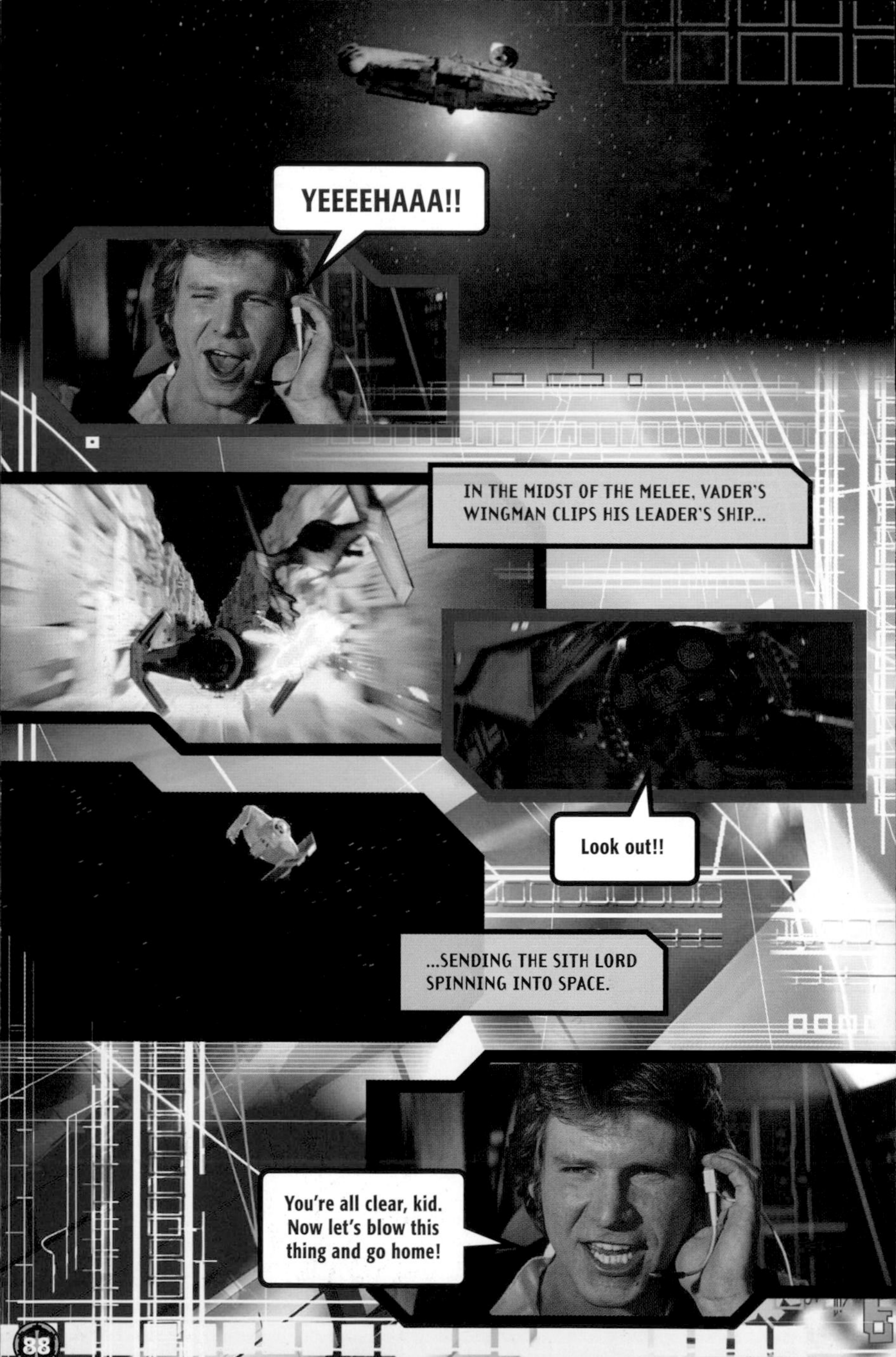
YEEEEHAAA!!
IN THE MIDST OF THE MELEE, VADER'S WINGMAN CLIPS HIS LEADER'S SHIP...
Look out!!
...SENDING THE SITH LORD SPINNING INTO SPACE.
You're all clear, kid. Now let's blow this thing and go home!

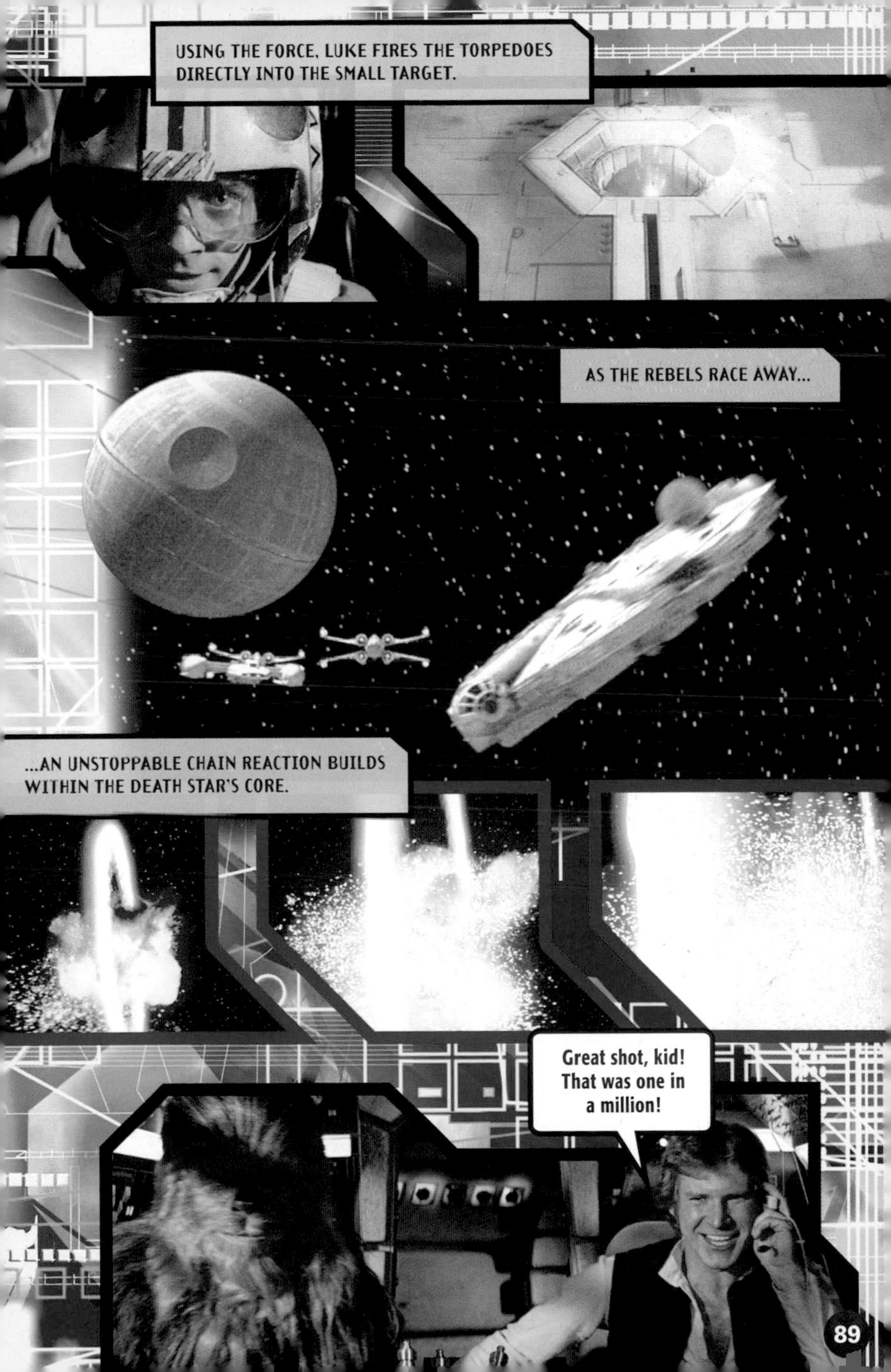
USING THE FORCE, LUKE FIRES THE TORPEDOES DIRECTLY INTO THE SMALL TARGET.
AS THE REBELS RACE AWAY...
...AN UNSTOPPABLE CHAIN REACTION BUILDS WITHIN THE DEATH STAR'S CORE.
Great shot, kid! That was one in a million!

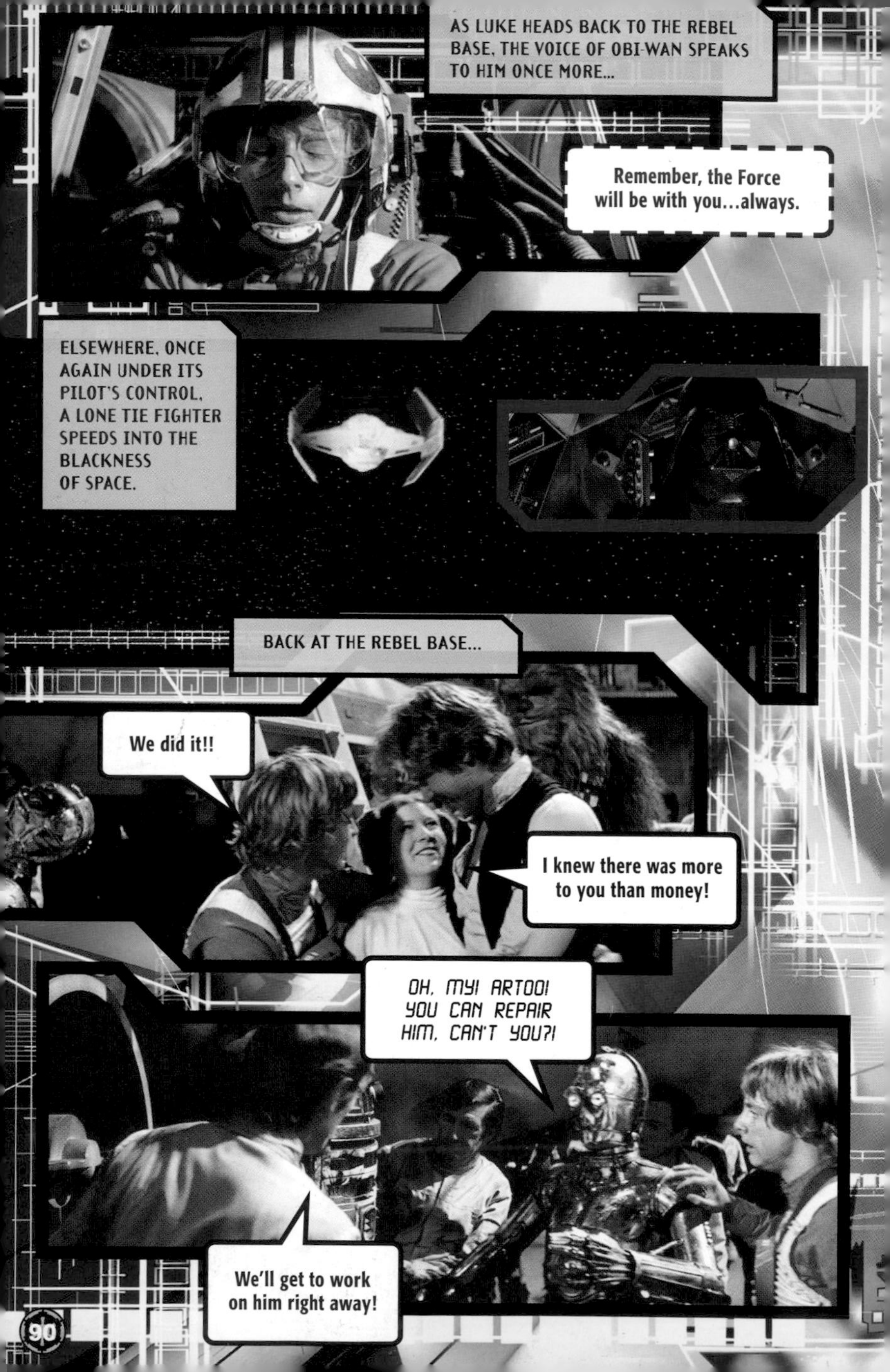
AS LUKE HEADS BACK TO THE REBEL BASE, THE VOICE OF OBI-WAN SPEAKS TO HIM ONCE MORE...
Remember, the Force will be with you...always.
ELSEWHERE, ONCE AGAIN UNDER ITS PILOT'S CONTROL, A LONE TIE FIGHTER SPEEDS INTO THE BLACKNESS OF SPACE.
BACK AT THE REBEL BASE...
We did it!!
I knew there was more to you than money!
OH, MY! ARTOO! YOU CAN REPAIR HIM, CAN'T YOU?!
We'll get to work on him right away!

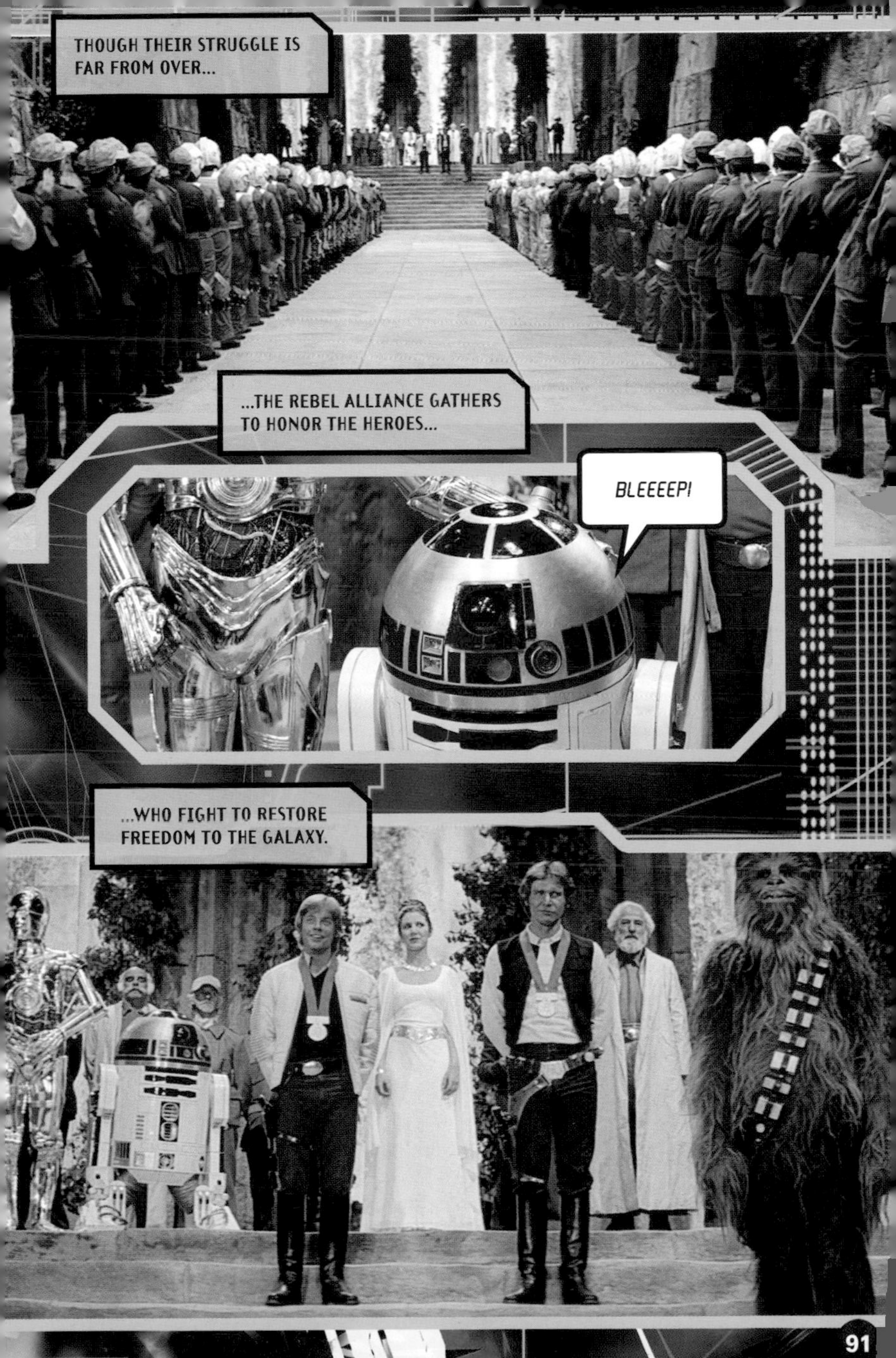
THOUGH THEIR STRUGGLE IS FAR FROM OVER...
...THE REBEL ALLIANCE GATHERS TO HONOR THE HEROES...
BLEEEEP!
...WHO FIGHT TO RESTORE FREEDOM TO THE GALAXY.

BEHIND THE SCENES

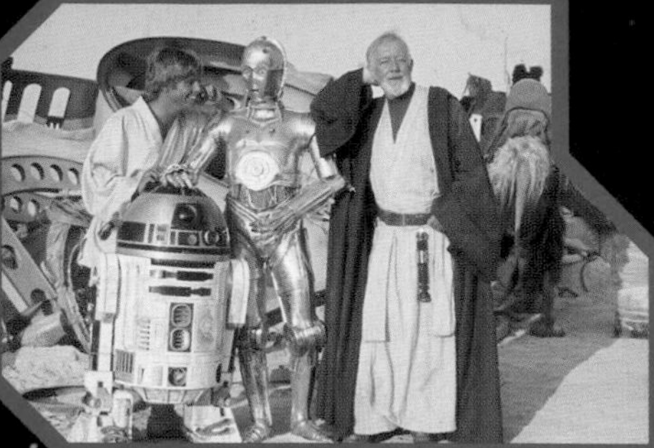

Alec Guinness (Obi-Wan Kenobi) clowning around on location.

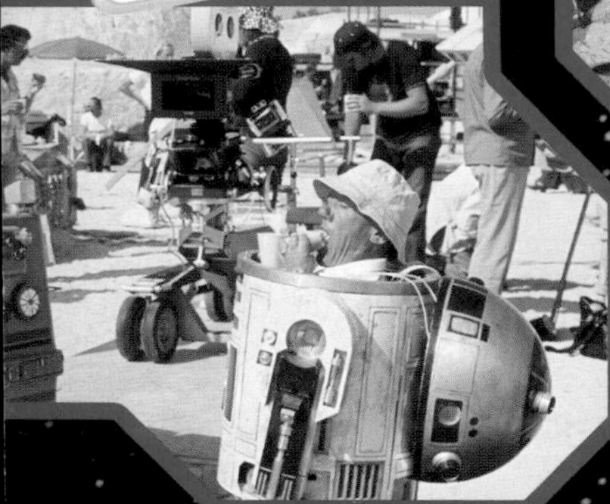

Kenny Baker (R2-D2) breaks for lunch.

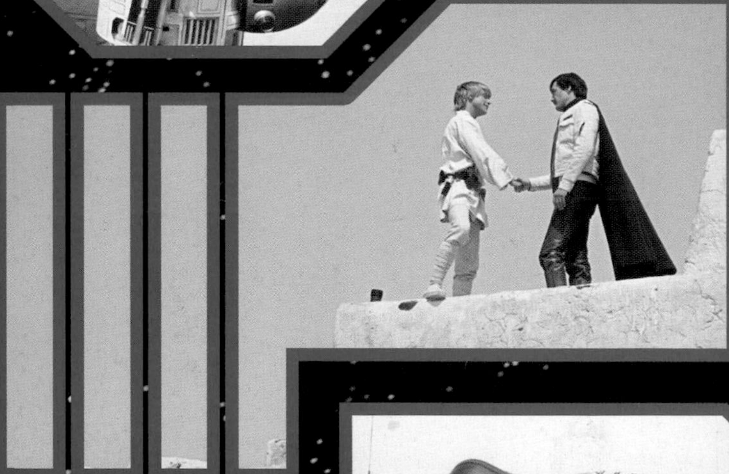

Still from the deleted scene where Biggs (Garrick Hagon) tells Luke (Mark Hamill) that he intends to join the Rebels.

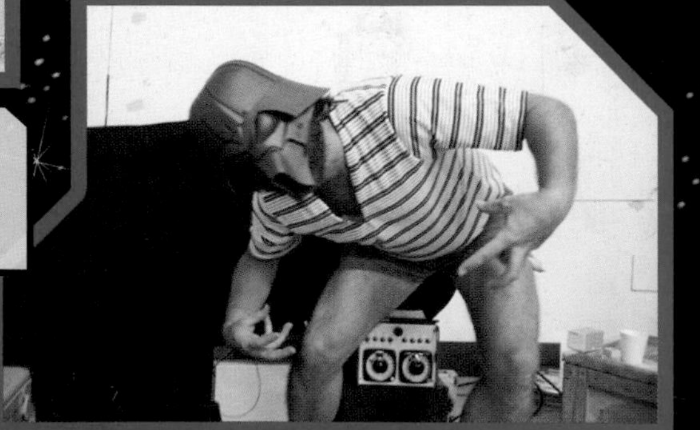

David Prowse (Darth Vader) tries on an early prototype helmet.

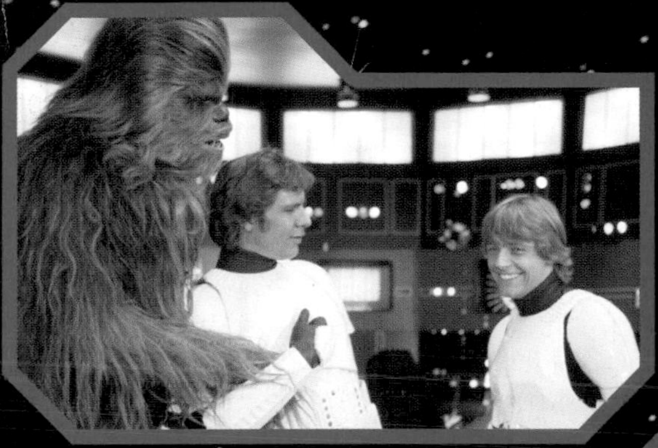

Peter Mayhew (Chewbacca), Harrison Ford (Han Solo) and Mark Hamill (Luke Skywalker) share a humorous moment.

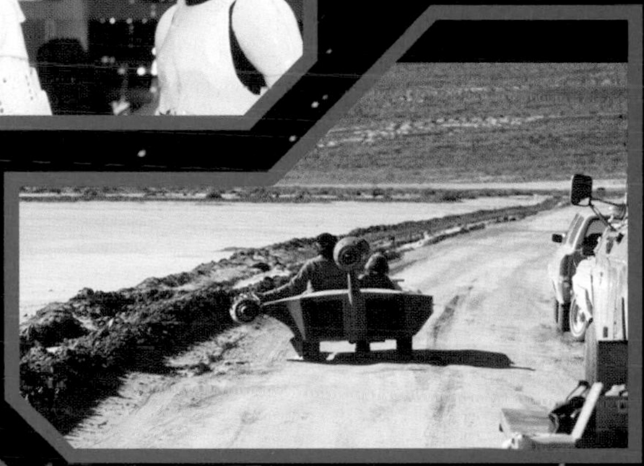

The REAL Landspeeder.

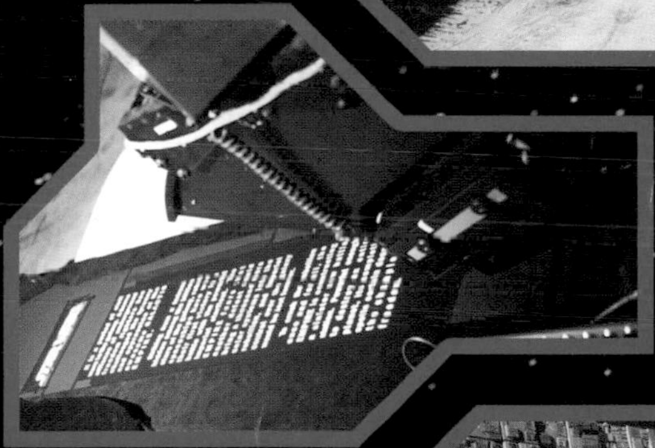

Track camera shooting the opening prologue.

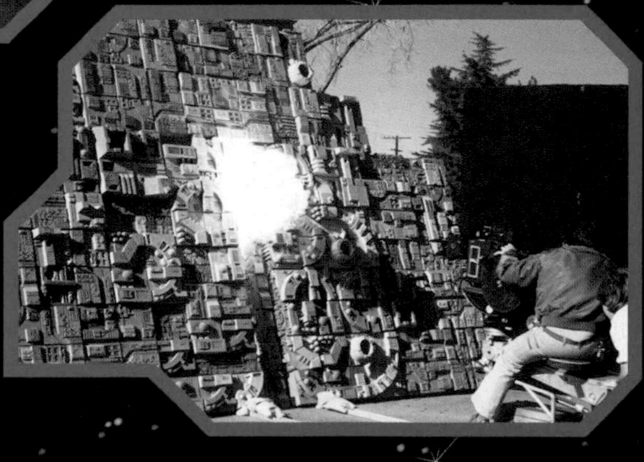

The crew of Industrial Light & Magic shooting a miniature explosion for the Death Star battle sequence.

BEHIND THE SCENES

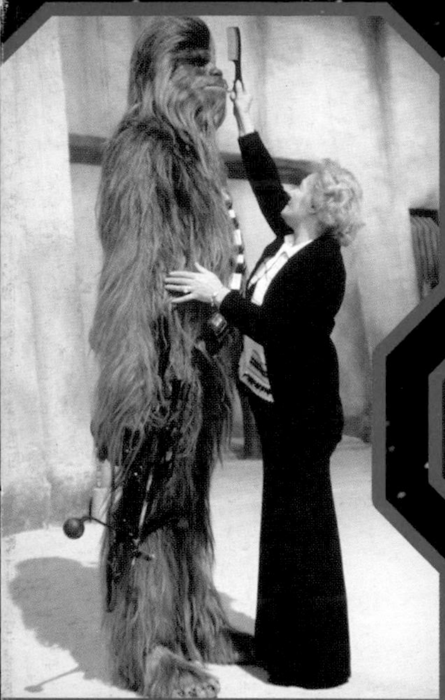

Peter Mayhew (Chewbacca) gets some last-minute grooming.

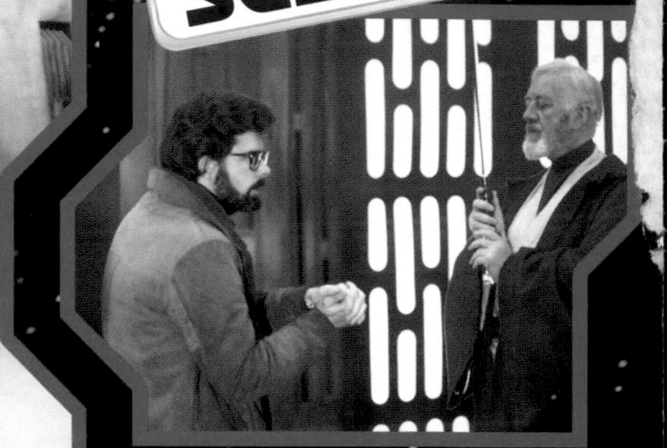

George Lucas compares lightsaber techniques with Alec Guinness (Obi-Wan Kenobi).

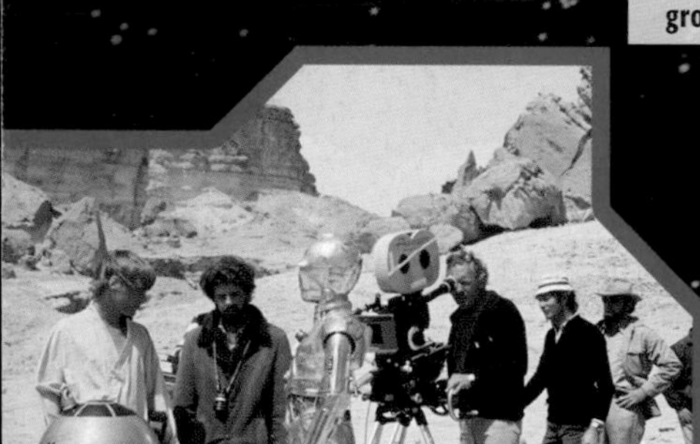

Kenny Baker (R2-D2), Mark Hamill (Luke Skywalker), George Lucas and Anthony Daniels (C-3PO) on location in Tunisia.

Crew members assist Anthony Daniels (C-3PO).

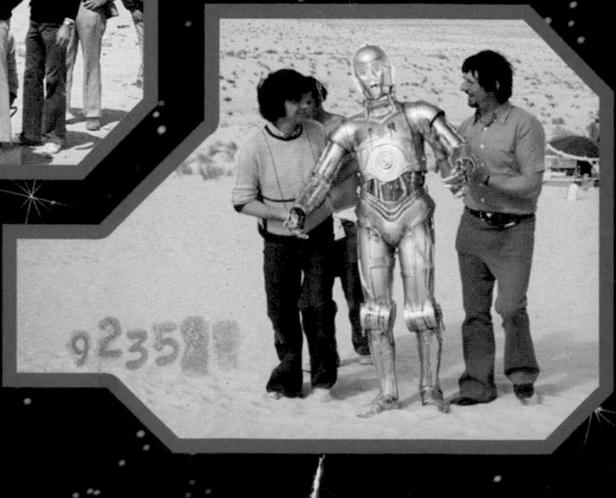
9235

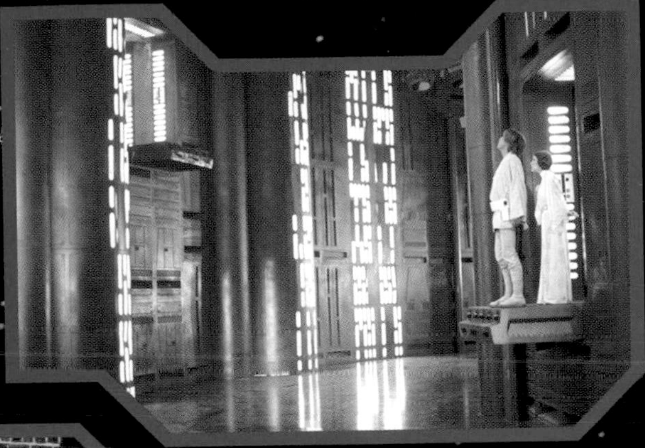

Mark Hamill (Luke Skywalker) and Carrie Fisher (Princess Leia) prepare to swing across the chasm...before the visual effects are added in.

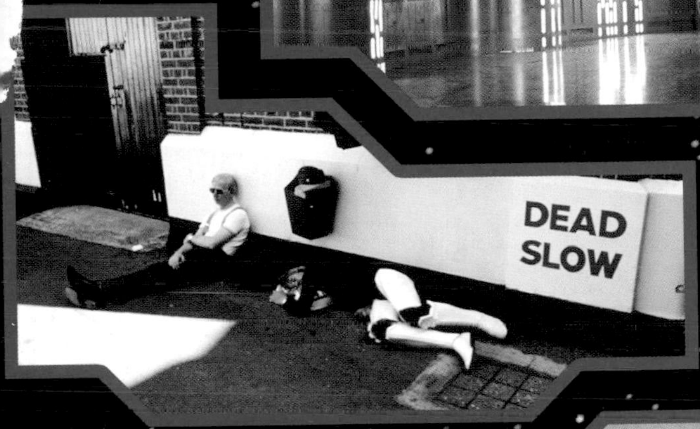
DEAD
SLOW

A stormtrooper takes a nap break outside the set.

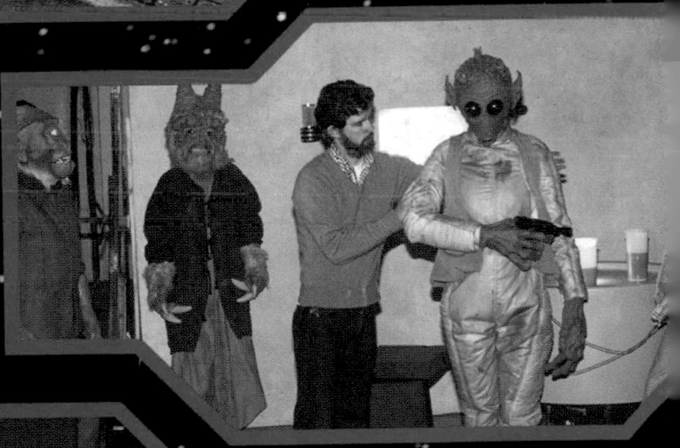

George Lucas and Greedo on the cantina set.

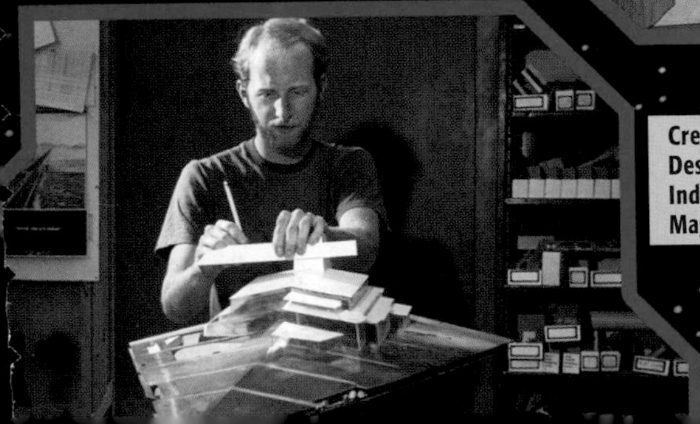

Creating a Star Destroyer model at Industrial Light & Magic.

STAR WARS GRAPHIC NOVEL TIMELINE (IN YEARS

Tales of the Jedi—5,000–3,986 BSW4
Knights of the Old Republic—3,964 BSW4
Jedi vs. Sith—1,000 BSW4
Jedi Council: Acts of War—33 BSW4
Prelude to Rebellion—33 BSW4
Darth Maul—33 BSW4
Episode I: The Phantom Menace—32 BSW4
Outlander—32 BSW4
Emissaries to Malastare—32 BSW4
Jango Fett: Open Seasons—32 BSW4
Twilight—31 BSW4
Bounty Hunters—31 BSW4
The Hunt for Aurra Sing—30 BSW4
Darkness—30 BSW4
The Stark Hyperspace War—30 BSW4
Rite of Passage—28 BSW4
Jango Fett—27 BSW4
Zam Wesell—27 BSW4
Honor and Duty—24 BSW4
Episode II: Attack of the Clones—22 BSW4
Clone Wars—22–19 BSW4
Clone Wars Adventures—22–19 BSW4
General Grievous—20 BSW4
Episode III: Revenge of the Sith—19 BSW4
Dark Times—19 BSW4
Droids—3 BSW4
Boba Fett: Enemy of the Empire—2 BSW4
Underworld—1 BSW4
Episode IV: A New Hope—SW4
Classic Star Wars—0–3 ASW4
A Long Time Ago . . . —0–4 ASW4
Empire—0 ASW4
Rebellion—0 ASW4
Vader's Quest—0 ASW4
Boba Fett: Man with a Mission—0 ASW4
Jabba the Hutt: The Art of the Deal—1 ASW4
Splinter of the Mind's Eye—1 ASW4
Episode V: The Empire Strikes Back—3 ASW4
Shadows of the Empire—3–5 ASW4
Episode VI: Return of the Jedi—4 ASW4
X-Wing Rogue Squadron—4–5 ASW4
Mara Jade: By the Emperor's Hand—4 ASW4
Heir to the Empire—9 ASW4
Dark Force Rising—9 ASW4
The Last Command—9 ASW4
Dark Empire—10 ASW4
Boba Fett: Death, Lies, and Treachery—11 ASW4
Crimson Empire—11 ASW4
Jedi Academy: Leviathan—13 ASW4
Union—20 ASW4
Chewbacca—25 ASW4
Legacy—130 ASW4

Old Republic Era
25,000 – 1000 years before
Star Wars: A New Hope

Rise of the Empire Era
1000 – 0 years before
Star Wars: A New Hope

Rebellion Era
0 – 5 years after
Star Wars: A New Hope

New Republic Era
5 – 25 years after
Star Wars: A New Hope

New Jedi Order Era
25+ years after
Star Wars: A New Hope

Legacy Era
130+ years after
Star Wars: A New Hope

Infinities
Does not apply to timeline

Sergio Aragonés Stomps Star Wars
Star Wars Tales
Star Wars Infinities
Tag and Bink
Star Wars Visionaries

9235038

BSW4 = before *Episode IV: A New Hope*. ASW4 = after *Episode IV: A New Hope*.